New York City of Trees

BENJAMIN SWETT

New York City of Trees

The Quantuck Lane Press | New York

New York City of Trees
Benjamin Swett

Text and photographs copyright © 2013 by Benjamin Swett

Design by Laura Lindgren
Map by Myra Klockenbrink
Manufacturing through Asia-Pacific Offset

ISBN: 978-1-59372-052-0

frontispiece: Tuliptree *Liriodendron tulipfera* 76" (page 106)

Publication of this book was partially underwritten by a grant
from Furthermore: a program of the J. M. Kaplan Fund,
with the support of the City Parks Foundation.

The Quantuck Lane Press | New York
www.quantucklanepress.com

Distributed by
W. W. Norton & Company
500 Fifth Avenue, New York, NY 10110
www.wwnorton.com

W. W. Norton & Company Ltd.,
Castle House, 75/76 Wells Street, London, WIT 3QT

1 2 3 4 5 6 7 8 9 0

For Katherine, Nicky, and Willie

and in memory of dear Rachel

Contents

Introduction

There is a stand of trees in a village in Iran that is thought to grow on "living memory." The villagers have revered and protected the trees for generations in the belief that cutting them would be bad luck. They call the trees *rahmani*, or "god's gift." Botanists have studied these trees because they grow at a higher altitude (1,730 m) than that at which the species (Caucasian wingnut, or *Pterocarya fraxinifolia*; see page 30) usually thrives. There have been calls for national protection for the trees and even designation as a National Natural Monument. I mention the trees, however, not because of their interest to science but because of what they suggest about trees and memory. It is common to talk about how trees improve living conditions in cities by filtering and cooling the air, absorbing excess rainwater, and making neighborhoods more attractive, but little has been said about the equally important role of trees as storehouses of a city's past. Just as trees remove carbon from the atmosphere and hold it for many years in their woody tissue, so do they sequester the shared experiences of the people who live alongside them. In meaningful ways, trees carry on the collective memories of communities.

Part of everything we exhale, whether from our lungs, from our chimneys, or from the exhaust pipes of our cars, is absorbed by a tree and stored away in a layer of wood. Like the strata of soil that archaeologists dig down through to find evidence of earlier civilizations, the growth rings of trees contain, in organized fashion, physical manifestations of the world and of the human presence in it at different times in a tree's history. By studying the ratios of carbon in tree rings, for example, scientists have been able to chart the increasing use of fossil fuels by humans over the centuries. Years of great fires, floods, logging—any dramatic changes, really, in the vicinity of a tree, whether caused by nature or by man—are recorded in measurable ways in the rings. Even the ordinary things—the average years, when nothing unusual happens—are kept as well in the wood that forms. Tuliptrees still growing at George Washington's house in Virginia, which we know Washington planted in 1785, contain, in their rings, a record of what Mount Vernon was like in that year. In a similar way, the millions of trees in the parks, along the streets, and in the backyards and cemeteries of New York City collect and hold the city's past.

Trees also store memories through the associations they carry for the people who live alongside them and see them every day. This is what I have explored in this book. Because trees become what they are in response to genetics and the places where they grow; because, in cities, large numbers of people come to know and recognize particular trees over time; and because these trees live longer—sometimes much longer—than any of the people who see them they take on an emotional and psychological importance that is as significant as the more abstract kinds of information stored in the growth rings or the practical amenities provided by the wood and leaves. By looking at a group of trees I have known over many years, scattered around the five boroughs of New York City, I have tried to show how much of the life of New York is contained in its trees.

I first began to think about New York City as a place of trees around the time I began to photograph them, in the mid-1990s. I was working for the Parks Department then and the City Parks Foundation had asked me to write a brochure about the city's 120 Great Trees. I had requested permission to photograph the trees as well, and as I went around the city visiting the extraordinary specimens growing in different neighborhoods I found myself under constant surveillance by residents. People would stand and watch me set up the tripod and focus the lens and then begin asking questions and making comments. This was disconcerting at first, but eventually I realized that the comments and questions were forcing me to understand the trees in a different way. These large plants along the streets or in the parks or cemeteries excited people's imaginations; they had meanings for their human neighbors that were strong and personal and seemed to connect to something larger. People took pride in their trees and were hungry for concrete information about them.

At the ginkgo in Isham Park in northern Manhattan, for example (see page 98), a man began telling me how his grandfather had said that the tree had been growing there when he—the grandfather—was a boy, and how the grandfather had showed him, in the wall beneath the tree, one of the original milestones from when that stretch of Broadway was the Boston Post Road and carried postal riders to Boston. At the white oak at the ninth hole of the Split Rock Golf Course (page 122), one golfer began describing an even bigger oak he had known in his childhood in Alabama, and another recounted a somewhat confusing but essentially correct story about American soldiers hiding behind stone walls to escape the British during the American Revolution. As I stood there talking with people I had never met, and would probably never see again, I realized that I was standing not so much at a tree as at a busy intersection of people's lives.

The brochure for the City Parks Foundation turned into a book that was published in 2000 as *Great Trees of New York City: A Guide*. I kept photographing trees after that, not just the designated "great trees" but ordinary trees that interested me not so much for their size or age or species as for the stories they suggested. Sometimes the stories turned out to be about the trees themselves and how they came to be growing in that spot. If they were exotic specimens from the other side of the globe, their seeds or seedlings most probably had traveled an interesting route to end up growing old in Brooklyn or Queens. If they were the native oaks or tuliptrees that have flourished in these parts since before Henry Hudson arrived, architectural changes and historical events had often taken place around them during their lifetimes. Very often the stories were about the human neighbors of the trees or the histories of the communities in which the trees grew. Sometimes, too, the stories were about my own experiences visiting the trees. All of this seemed to amount to a kind of alternative narrative of the city—the story of the place seen slightly askew, as if through leaves and branches.

Whether they are aware of it or not, whether they like it or not, people in New York City exist in a relationship with trees. An estimated 5.2 million grow along the streets and in the parks, cemeteries, and backyards of the city. The existence of so many nonlocal species that we now take for granted—white mulberry, ginkgo, osage orange, dawn redwood, royal paulownia—is a direct or indirect result of human intervention and tells something about New Yorkers' ability to create and cope with change. In his authoritative account of changes on Manhattan Island since Henry Hudson explored the region, Eric Sanderson has written that, because of introductions, "the plant diversity of New York City today may be twice what it was in 1609." This diversity of plants is a reflection of the diversity of the human population and the regular intervention of humans in the ecology of the region.

Part of the appeal and power of these trees is how little one can ultimately know about them. You can identify the species from the leaves and bark; estimate the mass from the diameter, height, and crown spread; learn the age and something of the history from the growth rings—yet the life of each individual specimen remains a mystery. Most of us take for granted these everyday parts of the landscape and tend to ignore them until something happens to one we have known for many years. A limb falls, or the tree itself is removed because it is no longer safe or it interferes with somebody else's plans, and it is as if a hole has been cut, not so much in the city as in our understanding of the city. Trees are like safe deposit boxes in which people lock their most private perceptions. When a tree is removed it is as if someone has broken in and robbed you of something both priceless and of no value to anyone else.

Perhaps because we know so little about them, the trees also appeal to the imagination as witnesses of events of the past. As Todd Forrest of the New York Botanical Garden put it, trees "bear the scars of their lives." Not only through the woody layers inside them but through the more outwardly visible twists and bends in their trunks, the scars and fissures in their bark, and the stumps and holes of lost limbs do they show the influences of the places where they have grown and give back signs of what we ourselves have done to them. Every block in New York City has a scarred veteran, such as the elm on Bruckner Boulevard (page 36), but perhaps the most powerful example is the so-called Survivor Tree at the 9/11 Memorial in lower Manhattan. A Callery pear pulled from the wreckage after the collapse of the World Trade Center towers on September 11, 2001, and kept alive by the Parks Department before being replanted near its original location ten years later, the tree stands apart as the only one of its species among the 412 swamp white oaks planted at the site of the fallen buildings. Though growing healthily again the tree looks odd. You can't help but notice it. Everyone does. In more ways than one wants to imagine, the jarring tree contains a day in the life of every New Yorker born before the twin towers fell.

In his fascinating book *Forests: The Shadow of Civilization*, Robert Pogue Harrison points out how trees stand apart, mute and even frightening in their connections to forces outside our control. The state of the sidewalk under the elm on page 94 and the very existence of the ailanthus on page 72 illustrate how the urge of trees to live can be destructive to human order and safety. If you don't look after your trees, they will look after themselves. Not only in myths and fairy tales but also in national traditions of the American frontier, trees conjure up images and ideas of wild beasts, extremes of weather and terrain, the destruction of property, loneliness. The recent spate of lawsuits against New York City for injuries and even a death caused by falling branches is itself a reminder of the forces forests can unleash. We could respond to these threats by cutting down the trees. Or we could, like the villagers in Iran, recognize the value of trees as bearers of cultural memory and provide the Parks Department sufficient funds to take care of them.

In this book I have included the trees I know best, and I have tried to capture both their stories and the experience of visiting them. Inevitably in a book about a place, some species are represented more heavily than others. The heartrending forms and precarious conditions of the city's old English and American elms have always appealed to me, and I have more pictures of them than of any other species. I have also spent more time with trees closer to home. That my photographs of three in Central Park were all made on the same snowy morning in 2010 is linked directly to the ease with which I could carry my camera outside and shoot them while the snow was still falling.

Several of the trees have been lost since I photographed them. Storm and age took some, and human convenience others. Just days before this book went to the printer, one of the grandest old trees in the city, the white oak on the Split Rock Golf Course in Pelham Bay Park (page 122), met its end in Hurricane Sandy. With weather patterns changing and infrastructure improvement an ongoing force in urban life, it is likely that such losses will persist and the landscape will continue to shift in unexpected ways.

This is not a guidebook, although Myra Klockenbrink's lovely map (page 133) will point the curious in the right direction. Rather, it is a picture of the city as I know it, and this includes parts of it that have been lost as well as those that remain. The book is arranged not by geography or by species but by the photographs themselves and how they seem to relate to one another. Trees from all corners of the world grow around New York City according to their own order, which follows no easy political or botanical system but is unique to the larger ecosystem of which the trees are a part. Likewise I have allowed the book to have its own order, like a forest—or a city—where one loses one's way and then finds it again through particulars.

Please note: The measurements listed after the scientific names represent the standard forester's measurement of diameter at breast height (dbh) on the day the photograph was taken. The more I learn about trees the less faith I have in dbh as an indicator of a tree's age. Nevertheless, a succession of dbh measurements over a number of years can give a picture of a tree's growth or lack thereof over time. Dbh is the first measurement arborists take when they encounter a tree, much as pulse or temperature is the first a doctor might record with a person. It is a simple, quick way to describe a tree and distinguish it from others.

Camperdown Elm *Ulmus glabra 'Camperdownii'* 45.5"
Boathouse Lawn, Prospect Park, Brooklyn
October 15, 2009

As the story goes, one day around 1835 David Taylor, the forester for the earl of Camperdown in Dundee, Scotland, noticed a peculiar twisted elm branch wriggling along the ground in the forest at Camperdown House. Intrigued, he grafted the branch onto the trunk of a common Wych elm and watched patiently as the weird contorted form of a tree began to grow. (The branch, as is the case with any "weeping" variety of plant, lacked a gene for what is known as "negative geotropism"—the urge to grow upward.) In 1872 a florist from East New York, Brooklyn, who seems to have enjoyed donating plants to Prospect Park, gave the park a clone of the Camperdown elm grafted onto another Wych elm. The tree prospered, and by 1935 it was recorded on park plans to have a diameter of 27 inches and to be surrounded by a pipe-rail fence. The tree continued to grow and to be cared for by the gardeners of Prospect Park, but in the 1960s signs of stress began to appear. In 1967, with the city in financial decline and funds for parks beginning to dry up, a group calling itself the Friends of Prospect Park sent out a mailing soliciting funds for its care. The mailing was read by the poet Marianne Moore, who lived nearby in Fort Greene. That summer Moore published an article in the *New York Times* describing the plight of the tree, and in September her poem "The Camperdown Elm" appeared in *The New Yorker*. The poem imagined the "rapture" that Thomas Cole and "Thanatopsis-invoking tree-loving" William Cullen Bryant, standing "at the edge of a rockledge overlooking a stream" in Asher B. Durand's painting *Kindred Spirits*, would have felt on gazing at this tree, which she concluded by calling "our crowning curio." Critics have responded in different ways to this fund-raising plea by the eighty-year-old poet, but none has argued that the poem wasn't effective not only in raising money for fertilization, pruning, and cabling, but also in bringing the tree to the attention of the world. Thanks to Marianne Moore, this Camperdown elm is now, perhaps, as a single specimen, the most celebrated tree in Brooklyn (for more on Camperdown elms, see page 42).

Weeping Beech *Fagus sylvatica 'pendula'* 62"
Jay Gould Plot, Woodlawn Cemetery, Bronx
April 27, 2009

Woodlawn Cemetery was a "cold and dreary spot" on December 6, 1892, when the family and friends of Jay Gould gathered to lay him to rest beside his wife, Helen, in the small Greek temple he had built after her death in 1889. Writing for an audience apparently breathless with curiosity about every detail of the burial, a somewhat morbid reporter described "twenty catacombs altogether" inside the mausoleum, "ten on each side, in tiers of five," and concluded, "only the two catacombs have occupants now." One of the most unscrupulous, daring, and successful businessmen in American history, Gould amassed a fortune worth $72 million at the time of his death by taking over railroads and manipulating the gold market. We can't say for sure whether the weeping beech on the south side of his plot was already growing there when he joined his wife in the mausoleum, but it could not have been planted much later: in a 1914 photograph it was grown and a healthy tree. A specialized variety of the European beech (pages 38, 60, 110), the weeping beech was first imported to this country from Belgium by the Flushing nurseryman Samuel Bowne Parsons in 1847. According to the Parks Department, the original weeping beech "grew on a Belgian estate, but was ordered destroyed by its owner due to its odd shape. Luckily, the estate gardener saved the tree, and it became the genetic parent of every subsequent weeping beech." The specimen that Parsons first imported and planted on his property in Queens was declared a city landmark in 1966. By the time of its death, in 1998, the beech's low-hanging branches had sprouted a circle of offspring that continue to surround the empty spot where it grew. Parsons worked closely with the Central Park designers Frederick Law Olmsted and Calvert Vaux to supply trees for that and many other parks. One of his sons, Samuel Parsons Jr., became a partner of Vaux and was the head landscape architect of New York City from 1895 until 1911. With their extensive tree operations in Queens, the Parsons family retained a kind of monopoly hold on trees in New York City—just as Jay Gould had on railroads and gold.

Common Pear *Pyrus communis* 42"
Private Residence, Woodside, Queens
April 6, 2010

When Marian and Wolfgang Radermacher bought their house in 1965, Mr. Radermacher was working as a tool and die maker for the Bulova Watch Company of Woodside. They chose the house because it was in a good school district, was near Mr. Radermacher's place of work, and had a yard with a beautiful pear tree where their children could play. Now the children are grown up and have families of their own and Mr. Radermacher is retired. A large apartment building has been put up next door, but otherwise much is the same, especially for the pear tree, which continues to blossom and put forth fruit every year, as it always has. Nobody knows who planted it or how old it is but it remains as healthy and productive as ever, and the Radermachers say the fruit is delicious. Still attached to the trunk is the green plaque that the Parks Department commissioner Henry J. Stern hung on it in 1985, identifying it as one of the 120 Great Trees designated that year after a citywide "Great Tree Search." Fewer than one hundred of the trees remain, and of these almost none retains its plaque. The common pear is a quiet species, with little attention paid to it one way or another. Until recently, arborists in cities preferred the tougher Callery pear, whose upright growth pattern is more suited to streets (for more on Callery pears, see pages 68–70). For years, however, a famous common pear grew at the corner of Third Avenue and 13th Street in Manhattan. Brought from England on a ship by Peter Stuyvesant, the former governor-general of New Amsterdam, in 1667, and planted on what was then his *bowerie* or farm, it continued to bear fruit as the city changed around it for two hundred years, until 1867, when a collision between two drays (open-sided carts) on a stormy day knocked it irretrievably over. As long as the Radermachers' pear continues to live in this peaceful, safe yard, away from traffic, it is unlikely that such an accident will befall it, and it may continue putting forth fruit, leaves, and blossoms for two hundred years as well.

Osage Orange *Maclura pomifera* (not measured)
Olmsted-Beil House, 4515 Hylan Boulevard, Staten Island
November 15, 2011

When it was first purchased in 1685 by a minister of the Dutch Reformed Church, the lot of the Olmsted-Beil house stretched down to Lower New York Bay. Over subsequent centuries and decades, however, subdivisions reduced the property to its present 1.7 acres, reached up a narrow driveway shared with two other houses. The place is in fact hard to find among the shopping malls, fast-food outlets, and housing developments of Hylan Boulevard, but once there it is as if the rest of Staten Island falls back a step and you find yourself in a kind of arboreal time warp. It was while he was living here, from 1848 until 1859, that Frederick Law Olmsted discovered his vocation as a landscape architect and began developing his plan for Central Park, and still growing here, in wild half-tended profusion, are some of the first trees he planted as he began experimenting with the relationship of plants to the land: a black walnut (48 inches), a three-trunked ginkgo (78 inches), an osage orange (not measured), a horsechestnut (50 inches), and two cedars of Lebanon (38 inches and 42 inches). Olmsted moved on to Manhattan, marriage, and celebrity in 1859, but the trees stayed put and kept growing. The property on which they grew passed through a succession of owners before coming into the possession of Carlton Beil, a naturalist and environmental educator, in 1961. The Parks Department bought the house from Beil in 2006, and Mr. Beil's grandson Mark DeFillo continued on as caretaker. The house, whose basement dates back to the seventeenth century and which had undergone typical expansions and renovations during the following three centuries, is in poor condition and closed to visitors until the city can renovate it once more and open the property as a park. But none of this seems to have hurt the trees, which continue to spread out in their own ways, finding a lot to like in their limited space, a reminder, perhaps, of the youthful Olmsted and the ideas he might have had for them and for what they could become (for more on osage oranges as a species, see page 114).

White Oak *Quercus alba* 70"
Pelham Bay Park, Bronx
2002

With the recent losses of two other extraordinary white oaks (see pages 122 and 130), this one, in a patch of forest behind the war memorial in Pelham Bay Park, has taken the crown as the largest of its species in the city. Its obscure location in woods frequented more by people who seem to wish to escape attention than by those who wish to be seen seems at least partially responsible for its continued good health. Unlike the deteriorating white oak on the Split Rock Golf Course, which had undergone major pruning and cabling to try to save it and protect golfers, this one has been left comparatively untouched, with the result that the trees around it and its own multiple branches (including the dead ones, which have been allowed to remain in place in this isolated spot) help absorb the wind and mitigate tension. According to the ecologist Eric W. Sanderson, the white oaks were not the biggest or most plentiful trees when Henry Hudson arrived in 1609—that honor is reserved for the nearly extinct American chestnut—but they were important nonetheless, along with tulip-trees, hickories, maples, and other "dukes and counts and princes" of native forests. The near-eradication of the American chestnut by a blight in the early years of the twentieth century, however, elevated oaks—and in particular the slow-growing white oak—and tuliptrees as the largest and most dramatic of New York City's native trees. Encountering one suddenly as one turns the corner of a path brings to mind the original inhabitants of the Bronx forests, the Siwanoy, who washed acorns from trees like this to remove the tannic acid and then ground the acorns into flour. A rusted fence in another part of Pelham Bay Park encircles the former location of the "Treaty Oak," where the Siwanoy are said to have sold this land to Thomas Pell in 1654. That tree burned to the ground on April 8, 1906, apparently from a fire caused by a tossed cigarette or cigar. This tree continues to grow in its patch of forest behind the war memorial, seen by few but occasionally troubling those who know of it with an inescapable feeling of dissatisfaction with their ordinary lives.

Persian Parrotia *Parrotia persica* 44"
Kissena Park Historic Grove, Flushing, Queens
October 25, 2010

Although not the most dramatic example of the species in the city (one in the Brooklyn Botanic Garden takes the cake for this), the Persian parrotia in Kissena Park nevertheless achieves a moment of glory for about half an hour toward the close of each clear day, when the sun reaches under its canopy and under the canopies of the trees around it to light up, in an almost offhand way, its exquisitely mottled, slender trunks. The tree is one of the many curiosities that the Parks Department inherited when it acquired this section of the Samuel Parsons nursery from the Parsons family in 1906 (see page 110). Native to the Hyrcania region of Iran, and also known as Persian ironwood, the species was first introduced to the United States in 1880 at the Harvard Botanic Garden in Cambridge, Massachusetts. According to Robert G. Nicholson of the Arnold Arboretum, "Most of the older specimens of *Parrotia* growing in the United States probably trace their lineage back to the Harvard plant." Although this specimen is shown on 1935 and 1936 maps of Kissena Park, little else is known about it. Whether, sometime before Samuel Parsons's death in 1906, the nursery acquired it through the Harvard lineage or came by it through some other means we can not say. All we know for sure is that, toward the close of each clear day, the sun manages to get under its leaves and under the leaves of the trees around it, and the four trunks shine forth unexpectedly, revealing themselves with a delicateness that probably goes unnoticed by the bicyclists, Rollerbladers, and runners who zoom through the park at that time, intent on exercise. As with the American hornbeam (page 56), the colloquial name "ironwood" derives from the hard, sinuous, muscular wood of the narrow trunks. As with the American sycamore (pages 34 and 50) and lacebark pine (page 46), the bark flakes off as the tree grows, creating the distinct camouflage look. It is named for the German-born naturalist Friedrich W. Parrot.

Caucasian Wingnut *Pterocarya fraxinifolia* 111"

Brooklyn Botanic Garden
October 29, 2009

The idea that tree age could bear any relation to trunk diameter falls apart when one considers the Caucasian wingnut at the Brooklyn Botanic Garden. One of the most photographed trees in the city, this three-trunked giant is a member of the Juglandaceae, or walnut, family and is native to Georgia, Azerbaijan, Armenia, Iran, and Turkey—not a tree you'd expect to find in Brooklyn. Its name derives from the semicircular *wings* that attach to nuts clustering along multitudinous hanging spikes. In the mountains of Iran it has been known as "God's gift" and thought to grow on "living memory" (see Introduction). The species was first introduced to France by the botanical explorer André Michaux in 1782 and planted at Versailles. The immense girth of this one qualifies it as one of the biggest trees in the city, yet according to garden records it was planted in just 1922, not even a hundred years ago. Of course, no tree in a city could ask for better growing conditions than those in the Brooklyn Botanic Garden, and it may be that, as with a few nonnative species, this one has an aggressive gene that programs it to luxuriate in our local circumstances. But all this only further supports the idea that, from an arboreal as well as human standpoint, surfaces are deceiving, and the biggest trees aren't necessarily the oldest. According to Chris Roddick, the arborist at the Brooklyn Botanic Garden, the tree has reached mature size and is already entering the state of existence known as *senescence*, in which organisms begin to reduce themselves and change their habits to cope better with the stresses of their environments. The tree has large cavities and wounds, "many of which are completely hollow," Mr. Roddick says, and is "in a constant battle trying to grow wood around these defects before they weaken the tree too much." Outside the frame of the picture one of the limbs is supported with a brace. Cared for by the Brooklyn Botanic Garden, the tree may continue to look as it does for a long time. In the wild it would certainly be less lucky. I like to think of this giant in relation to the tiny post oaks in Pelham Bay Park (page 118), so much smaller but so much older!

Cucumber Magnolia *Magnolia acuminata* 59"
Private Residence, Riverdale, Bronx
May 4, 2010

It seems reasonable to think that this cucumber tree was planted by William E. Dodge Jr. sometime around 1863, during the construction of Greyston, his stone house overlooking the Hudson River in Riverdale. Dodge was the son of a cofounder of the copper mining firm Phelps Dodge, and his 14,000-square-foot Gothic Revival granite mansion, designed by James Renwick Jr., remained in his family until 1961, when his grandson Cleveland Dodge donated the huge house to Columbia's Teachers College and moved into a smaller house he had built on a separate parcel nearby. Included in that other parcel was this cucumber tree, and ever since the tree has been legally attached to the smaller house (located to the left of the tree outside the frame of the picture). Greyston passed from Teachers College to a Buddhist organization in 1980, and then returned to private hands in 1988. The smaller house was purchased from Cleveland Dodge's estate by Gilbert Kerlin, a lawyer who during the 1950s had helped save sections of Riverdale from housing development and in 1960 had helped persuade the owners of Wave Hill to deed the historic estate overlooking the Hudson to the city. So strongly did Mr. Kerlin feel about the cucumber tree just up the hill from his house that, in 2001, when he remarried after his first wife died, his marriage ceremony took place under the tree. Also known as yellow flower magnolia, this massive, broad-spreading, flowering hardwood is the largest of the native magnolias and has the broadest range, from Florida to Ontario. The "cucumber" in the name derives from the shape of the small fruits that form after the petals of its orange-yellow flowers have dropped. For many years I looked for this tree in the woods of the Catskills and the Adirondacks but later learned that its native region is farther west in New York State.

American Sycamore *Platanus occidentalis* 62"

Conference House Park, Tottenville, Staten Island
February 5, 2010

On September 11, 1776, John Adams, Benjamin Franklin, and Edward Rutledge met briefly with Admiral Lord Richard Howe of the British navy in the stone house behind where this American sycamore now grows. American independence had been declared just two months previously, and Lord Howe was prepared to offer amnesty to certain Americans (not John Adams) if they would agree to lay down their arms. The meeting turned out a failure from the British standpoint, but it happened that, on the way to it, at a crowded New Jersey inn, Franklin and Adams had to share a bed in a very small room. Adams tried to close the window because he was "afraid of the evening air," but Franklin, who had published a theory on the benefits of fresh air while sleeping, insisted on leaving it open. As the historian David McCullough writes in *John Adams*, Franklin and Adams "lay side by side in the dark, the window open, Franklin expounding, as Adams remembered, 'upon air and cold and respiration and perspiration, with which I was so much amused that I soon fell asleep.' " As my family knows, this is one of my favorite anecdotes of the founding fathers, and I mention or think of it whenever I visit the American sycamore at the Conference House, though it is highly doubtful the sycamore was already growing here when the event took place. With their greenish-brown bark that flakes off as the trees grow, leaving white patches beneath, and their seed balls that can remain hanging on the branches even in winter, sycamores are a quintessential American tree, growing along streams and in fields from the east coast to the edge of the great plains, and from Maine to Florida. Like white oaks and tuliptrees, they are among the grandest of the native trees that still flourish in the United States and can live to a great age. The country's champion sycamore has a diameter of 134 inches. The specimen growing out back of the Conference House is less than half this size, yet it is one of the biggest in the city and, with its downspreading trunk and fast-closing cavity, one of the most visually and historically suggestive (another is on page 50).

American Elm *Ulmus americana* 37.5"
Bruckner Boulevard between Willis and Alexander Avenues, Bronx
May 14, 2009

This section of Bruckner Boulevard is one of the most heavily trafficked in the Bronx, especially in the morning when cars, trucks, and delivery vans back up as far as Willis Avenue to wait for the light at the entrance to the Third Avenue Bridge. Despite the surge of vehicles and the damage they have done to the American elm arching over them—especially the trucks that graze the trunk while parking to make pickups or deliveries at the antiques stores along the block—the tree remains remarkably healthy. Its survival, continuously threatened not only by trucks and cars but also by Dutch elm disease, from which it remains isolated but if not treated with fungicides unprotected, is one of those anomalies that call into question everything one takes for granted about trees in a city. For example, in New York builders have the right to petition the city to cut down street trees that interfere with construction plans in exchange for the payment of a restitution fee based on the size, species, and condition of the tree to be removed (see page 70). The idea is that, in exchange for the loss of the old tree, a sufficient number of new ones can be planted to equal the value of the old one. But in a city like New York, where a tree such as this will grow in public view, adapting to the space in which it has found itself, collecting the glances of strangers who drive underneath it or of neighbors who look up at it every day, longer than any of the people who see it will live, such calculations seem insufficient. How can a mathematical formula take into account how much a tree can come to mean to someone over time, or for how many people it can come to acquire such significance? How can a formula calculate the overall effect of a tree such as this, the only large one left on a busy boulevard in the South Bronx, on the place where it grows? Just the time it takes for a tree to achieve a certain size, year in and year out adding layer after layer of wood in response to the world as it presents itself at any given time, like a scribe piling up sheets of paper in an ongoing description of the events of each year, is difficult for most of us even to grasp.

European Beech *Fagus sylvatica* 49.5"

Raoul Wallenberg Forest, Riverdale, Bronx
April 2, 2009

The cat face crudely spray-painted onto this European beech—visible in the wet patch from the previous night's rain—is a reminder of the feral cats that for many years have made this wild bit of Bronx woods their home. On the day I took the picture, an array of rudimentary "houses"—plastic file boxes with holes cut in their sides—had been left at the back of the park by neighbors concerned about the untamed, born-in-the-wild cats that seem to proliferate here. In the 1980s a developer submitted a plan to build twenty-eight houses on the 4.37-acre piece of land. Intense neighborhood opposition and a couple of years of wrangling during the Koch administration led the succeeding Dinkins administration to buy the property and give it to the Parks Department in 1990. Among arguments in its favor as a park was that U Thant, the secretary-general of the United Nations from 1961 until 1971, had lived in the grand house that once stood here. The house had been one of the grandest of Riverdale, a mansion built during the 1890s by a copper-mining engineer and businessman named James Douglas, a president at Phelps Dodge and partner of fellow Riverdale resident William E. Dodge Jr. (see page 32). The mansion was demolished in 1974, and the Parks Department now maintains the grown-over property as a forest. Numerous large native trees—white oaks, black oaks, red oaks, tuliptrees—thrive here, and also some imported specimens planted by Douglas, including this European beech with the cat face spray-painted onto it. Behind the tree is the Hudson River, and behind that the Palisades and the rest of America, a view once regarded daily by Secretary-General U Thant but now obscured by the younger trees that have grown up in it. The thin gray bark of beeches invites carving and has long been associated with writing. It is rare to find one in the city in which people have not cut their names. The English word "book" derives from *boc*, Anglo-Saxon for "beech." In England the earliest books were sewn tablets of beech. The use of spray paint here seems somewhat sad, yet it maintains this history of beeches as transmitters of lore.

Royal Paulownia *Paulownia tomentosa* 71"

New York Botanical Garden, Bronx

May 14, 2009

One of the most noticeable trees in the New York Botanical Garden, or anywhere else in New York City, especially in May when its blossoms stand out against the varying greens around it, is this tree of paradox, the royal paulownia, valued for its color and form yet reviled by many as an invasive species that takes over ecosystems and pushes out native plants with its tough, fast-growing roots and branches (see page 80). Like the ailanthus (page 72) and the porcelainberry shrub, the royal paulownia is on all of the botanical watch lists, yet for a long time it was happily planted in American gardens, and landscapers and gardeners paid homage to it in field and book. As the story goes, its fat, lightweight seeds made a favored packing material for exports from China. These seeds slipped from crates and fell to the sides of railroad tracks in the United States and else-where and formed colonies that spread. The one here lost a large limb in 2008, giving the upper part an unusually slender look. Another large example beside the chapel at Sailors Snug Harbor on Staten Island (not in this book) demon-strates the massive hulking look the trees achieve when they get older. In one way the trees are not designed to grow older, and what we are seeing here is an anomaly: in its native China, paulownia is a transition species that dies off as soon as the next succession of trees grows up around it. It very often plays this same role in the United States, serving as a "pioneer" in places damaged by strip mining or cleared for overhead transmission lines. As Todd Forrest of the New York Botanical Garden pointed out to me, this specimen, like all non-native species in the garden, was planted deliberately, and horticulturists have cared for it as a unique example of the plant. In recent years, paulownia, also known as princess tree and foxglove tree, has begun occurring spontaneously in other parts of the garden, including the fifty-acre forest, and is no longer being planted. People continue to regard *Paulownia tomentosa* highly in many places. A type of clog in China and certain Japanese instruments can only be made of its strong, lightweight wood.

Camperdown Elm *Ulmus glabra 'Camperdownii'* 28.5"

Green-Wood Cemetery, Brooklyn

December 10, 2002

As is evident from the sudden change in color on the trunk, Camperdown elms are always grafted trees, composed of a clone of the original mutant branch from Camperdown House in Scotland grafted onto the trunk of an ordinary Wych elm. (Wych elm, *Ulmus glabra*, is also known as Scots elm.) Art Presson, the superintendent of grounds at Green-Wood Cemetery, doesn't know when this specimen was planted, but as it appears to be the second-largest of its kind in the city it was probably put in the ground not long after its more famous sibling in Prospect Park (see page 18). Camperdown elms became a somewhat fashionable tree to plant in graveyards in England and the United States during the second half of the nineteenth century, perhaps because their contorted, pendant branches appealed to Victorian tastes. Like Woodlawn Cemetery in the Bronx, Green-Wood is one of the finest aboretums in New York, with approximately 7,800 trees, many of them among the oldest in the city, carefully planted around its 478 acres. The cemetery opened in 1838, and by 1853 Manhattanites were so entranced by the peace and beauty of its parklike grounds that they began flocking here by the boatload for picnics. It is widely understood that the popularity of Green-Wood helped inspire the creation of Central Park in Manhattan. Picnics are no longer permitted, yet after 175 years the grounds are more parklike than ever. Staff tend to the trees, shrubs, and walks as carefully as they do to the monuments, and warblers, tanagers, orioles, and other birds flock here during their spring and fall migrations. Not far from the Camperdown elm, on a knoll covered with small marble gravestones, with unforgettable views back to Manhattan, is the highest point in Brooklyn—one of the reasons planners chose the site for the cemetery in the first place. When I first came here in 1996 with Fiona Watt, then a junior forester at the Parks Department, Fiona pointed out how much lichen was growing on the trunks of the trees. "Very picturesque," I said. "Actually, it means that the air quality is good here," she answered. It still is.

English Elm *Ulmus procera* 52" (partially removed 2005)
Madison Square Park, Manhattan
March 4, 2003

Madison Square was opened as a public park in 1847, and it is likely that this English elm dates from that time. The tree is one of a grove of seven English elms that have been growing in the park for as long as anyone can remember, four of which have been lost. Extensive paving may have damaged the roots of this one, which at some point curled back around each other and around the trunk in a process known as girdling. Or old age may just have begun getting the better of it. The tree started to fail and Parks Department arborists kept pruning it to try to save it. It was still failing when I took the picture in 2003, and not long afterward, for safety reasons, Parks removed all but the central shaft. Today the shaft, gray and brittle, remains standing in the park as a monument to an era when English elms were planted throughout New York City. Two hundred years ago this magnificent tree of the Boston Common found its way into most parks and was regularly planted along streets and in gardens. It was a standard offering in the catalogue of the Prince Nurseries of Flushing in 1822. By the middle of the nineteenth century, however, horsechestnuts and osage oranges—species especially prized by Frederick Law Olmsted, the codesigner of Central Park—had become the favored trees, and by the end of that century it was the American elm, planted up and down city streets as it was in towns across America. In the 1930s and '40s, under Parks Department commissioner Robert Moses, the London plane had its turn. And during the 1970s and '80s the Callery pear and the Norway maple gained prominence. Often overplanted in monocultures of a single type of tree, some of these species later turned out to have one problem or another, for example the Dutch elm disease that plagued American elms. But many, like this English elm, remained growing where they had been originally planted, maintaining their traditional forms surrounded by changing architecture and plants. When the Empire State Building was completed in 1931, this tree was already a stately specimen with a diameter of nearly 36 inches.

Lacebark Pine *Pinus bungeana* 30.5"
Wave Hill, Riverdale, Bronx
April 3, 2009

For its first thirty or forty years, this rare Chinese pine is more noticeable for its dense outer form than for the muscular spreading of its limbs or the camouflage patterns of its greenish-gray bark. Quickly glanced at in a backyard, a young specimen might be confused with any number of other species. But given half a human lifetime the tree, entering its own adolescence, begins to reveal more individual character. Charles Day, the horticultural interpreter at Wave Hill, could not say anything more about the age of this one than that it was definitely planted before 1960, when the garden and cultural center became public and records began to be kept. Its diameter is just slightly larger than that of a specimen at the New York Botanical Garden that we know to have been planted in 1909. Though shaded by an extremely tall American elm, and surrounded by dense clusters of bottlebrush buckeye (*Aesculus parviflora*), this tree, still very young by the records of its species, is growing at great speed: between 1996 and 2010 its diameter grew 5.5 inches. One of my students remembered walking down an allee of lacebarks at the Forbidden City in Beijing. Some of the world's oldest living examples, said to be more than eight hundred years old, can be found in Beijing and elsewhere in their native China. Emperor Qianlong (1736–96) granted titles to some ancient lacebarks and even built an irrigation system for them that mystified workers in modern-day Beihai Park until a tree became sick and a team of gardeners traced the cause to a blockage in a tunnel. Unless weather patterns change considerably, it is unlikely that such an irrigation system will be necessary for the lacebark at Wave Hill. Annual precipitation in the Hudson Valley has increased markedly over the past one hundred or so years and is currently at record-breaking levels. The well-mulched soil around the tree, carefully maintained by Wave Hill's gardeners, is ideal for absorbing rain.

Tuliptree *Lioriodendron tulipfera*, 71"
Spuyten Duyvil, Riverdale, Bronx
April 2, 2009

A couple of months after this picture was taken, when the leaves had come out on the branches above and the blossoms were beginning to open, I met Tom Bird at a table he had set up on a hand-built stone terrace near this tuliptree in his yard. To say it is his yard is not completely accurate, as the tree grows in a lot just above and to the side of the one on which his house stands, but this other lot has been under the control of Tom Bird's family since 1964, and functions, more or less, as a kind of overgrown backyard. A tall, fit man of sixty-five, with alert blue eyes and a trimmed white beard, Mr. Bird explained to me, over nuts and juice, how it was his father, Junius Bird, an archaeologist at the Museum of Natural History, who had first noticed the tree when he bought the house in 1938. The lot in which the tree grows was then vacant, and when it came up for sale in 1964 Junius and a neighbor chipped in and bought it together, protecting the tree and their source of shade. After Junius died, in 1982, Tom continued to live in the family house, and when the neighbor died some years later Tom bought full ownership of the lot and the tree. Except for the stone terrace and a small path (not in the picture), both of which Tom himself built, and a couple of disintegrating storage boxes, the lot is a wild place of luxuriant undergrowth and other large trees, on a steep hillside overlooking the Hudson River. Without too much effort, it is possible to imagine looking out through the branches at the square-rigged sails of Henry Hudson's ship the *Halve Maen*, sailing up the river some four hundred years ago—though it would be a stretch to claim that the tuliptree was standing then. Tuliptrees, which were made into canoes by the local Indians, are remarkably fast growers, and, according to Tom Bird, it is more likely that this one is closer to two hundred years old. When one of the four subcrowns fell after a lightning strike in 1964, his father counted 144 rings. In 1983, after more lightning strikes, Tom installed two lightning rods. To say that the tree is meaningful to him is an understatement. It is an important part of his life, and it connects him to his father.

American Sycamore *Platanus occidentalis* 52.5"

2030 Corlear Avenue, Kingsbridge, Bronx

September 30, 2011

One of the oldest of its species remaining on a New York City street, this sycamore became famous in the early 1980s when a neighbor, Bruce Snowden, noticed it was in poor shape and managed to raise enough money to convince the city to break up the concrete around it and irrigate, fertilize, prune, and fence it. At a ceremony attended by a couple hundred people on June 18, 1983, Mayor Ed Koch attached a plaque to the tree, naming it "Sister Tree" in honor of Saint Francis of Assisi, and spoke about the importance of the tree in the neighborhood. In subsequent years, the plaque was vandalized and replaced three times, and in the late 1990s a developer bought the parking lot where the tree then grew from the church that owned it and announced plans to build a seven-story condo. "What's all the fuss over a big old ugly tree?" the developer, John Lese, was quoted in the *New York Times* as saying. Under pressure from Snowden, the *Riverdale Press*, and others, however, Lese ended up hiring an arborist and redesigning the building to make space for the tree. He sold the property and the new owners created a U-shaped courtyard around the tree, named the building Sycamore Court Condos, and added a silhouette of a sycamore as a decoration in the lobby. Rather than destroy the tree, they incorporated it. When the project was completed in 2011, three-bedroom apartments were offered starting at $599,000. Whenever I visit the tree, I run into Patrick or Philip O'Flynn, brothers about my age who have lived on the block since the 1960s and whose mother grew up there. According to the O'Flynns, a branch used to reach out over Corlear Avenue, but after a car fire in which a burning SUV scorched it the branch was removed. Whether—shaded as it is on three sides by the new building—the tree will continue to receive enough sunlight to keep growing is a question that the O'Flynns and other neighbors have often asked, and that only time will answer. One thing we know for sure is that those who live near the tree will continue to watch over it and report back on its condition, as if it truly were Sister Tree, as Ed Koch named it. (For more on sycamores, see page 34.)

American Elm *Ulmus americana* 44"

Ridge Boulevard at 72nd Street, Bay Ridge, Brooklyn
April 26, 2010

Most people know that, until the outbreak of Dutch elm disease in 1930 (see page 94), American elms, prized as much for their shape as for their speed of growth, adorned the streets of many towns across America. What few recall is that this species also lined Ridge Boulevard and other avenues in Bay Ridge, and so thickly that their interconnecting branches often brushed the tops of street-cars on the muddy roads beneath. One of the last and largest of these trees, or of any American elm still growing on a Brooklyn street, this one is a relic of a beautification program intended to attract new home buyers to a neighborhood whose reputation (as well as population) had been ravaged by outbreaks of yellow fever and cholera in the first half of the nineteenth century. A reporter in the August 14, 1873, *Brooklyn Daily Eagle* described numerous "improvements" then under way to make Bay Ridge "eagerly sought after by the business men of New York for suburban homes." Among these was an effort to drain "100 ponds and stagnant pools" on the southern side of the ridge that were thought to contribute to "malarial fevers" and "the shakes." "New avenues and streets have been opened and graded, and an immense number of trees have been planted to shade them." The name Bay Ridge itself was part of this effort to remold the public image of the area. The community had originally been known as Yellow Hook, because of the yellowish soil that the Dutch found when they first began settling here in the 1600s. But outbreaks of yellow fever caused by *Aedes aegypti* mosquitoes escaping from ships and settling in local water made the earlier name distasteful, and residents voted to adopt the new one in 1853. The "ridge" in the name memorialized the glacial ridge where this elm still grows, which commanded (and still commands from the windows of the houses behind the tree) views, as the writer described them in that 1873 article, of "the waters of New York Bay, the heights of Staten Island, and the state of New Jersey as far as the Orange Mountains." That the tree predates these houses is clear from its awkward position in relation to the driveway someone has put past it.

Sassafras *Sassafras albidum* 43.5", 41.5"
Green-Wood Cemetery, Brooklyn
May 24, 2011

With its mitten-shaped leaves and a scent in its bark that once flavored root beer, sassafras tends to reproduce through root suckers, resulting in a tree difficult to transplant and often growing in colonies of genetically identical individuals. When most people think of sassafras, they think of these thickets of saplings that spring up in newly opened woods and turn a brilliant orangey red in the fall, and not of the hardy specimens such as these two at Green-Wood Cemetery that sometimes manage to survive and grow into stout, shade-giving trees. The Green-Wood trees probably share a root system that was here when the cemetery opened in 1838, and the trees themselves could predate the cemetery as well. Of the mature sassafras I have measured in the city, they are the largest in diameter, though their size is also a product of their superior growing conditions. (While making their map of trees in Central Park, Ken Chaya and Ned Barnard found one in dense woods in the north end of the park that, though smaller in diameter than these two, exhibits other characteristics of a highly stressed ancient tree and probably predates that park.) The largest sassafras in the country, the national champion, in Owensboro, Kentucky, has a diameter of 88 inches. Among the graves scattered around these two is that of James Merritt Ives (1824–95), the marketing and bookkeeping half of the nineteenth-century artistic partnership Currier and Ives. The circle of stones behind the trees marks a plot owned by the Dutch Reformed Church of downtown Brooklyn. The stones were moved here after the church sold its Fulton Street burial ground in the 1840s. Like many other cemeteries, such as Woodlawn in the Bronx and Mount Auburn in Cambridge, Massachusetts, Green-Wood has helped preserve some of the region's oldest trees and, although the roots have unsettled or cracked gravestones and monuments over the years, the trees themselves have made the grounds more attractive and seem to serve as long-term guardians of those consigned there. (For more on Green-Wood, see page 42.)

American Hornbeam *Carpinus caroliniana* 147"
Boathouse Lawn, Prospect Park, Brooklyn
October 15, 2009

The American hornbeam is an understory tree, which means that mature specimens rarely grow out in the open on their own, or as the dominant species in a forest. They grow in the shade of mature forests and form thickets in old fields. Like its less crooked cousin the European hornbeam (see page 96), it develops a distinctive spreading shape in old age and can grow quite large in a park or arboretum. Its leaves turn a brilliant orangey red in the fall. Underneath its smooth, thin, bluish-gray bark its rippling wood is extremely hard. Foresters tend to call it "muscular." Settlers made mallets and tool handles from American hornbeam and named it ironwood. It is also known as blue beech because its bark is so beech-like. Because it often grows on slopes above streams, beavers find it handy. The specimen behind the Boathouse in Prospect Park is the largest in the city and perhaps the most beautiful in the world. The combined diameters of its three main trunks was 144 inches in 1996 and 147 inches in 2009. It is still growing, but slowly. Nobody who passes under it on the path to the Lullwater Bridge can fail to be affected by its multitudinous, broad-spreading, narrow branches. Just to the east of it, across a lawn, encircled by a fence, is Prospect Park's much-celebrated Camperdown elm (page 18). The hornbeam is mentioned alongside the Camperdown in an undated 1967 letter by Marianne Moore to M. M. Graff of the Friends of Prospect Park (quoted by Kirby Olson): "how delighted I am that the salvage of the great Elm is assured, and of the hornbeam . . . life is worth living when people have hearts!"

White Mulberry *Morus alba* 55"
Conference House Park, Tottenville, Staten Island
February 5, 2010

The general distaste among foresters for the white mulberry seems to stem partly from its aggressive character and partly from its ungainly form. Citing its "messy, unkempt appearance," the horticulturist Michael Dirr calls it "one of the original garbage can trees" and assigns it a landscape value of "none." In his *Natural History of New York City*, published in 1959, John Kieran preferred the "native Red Mulberry (*Morus rubra*), a sturdier and shaplier tree with a longer fruiting season." Homeowners, likewise, often disparage the tree for the squishy mess its fruit leaves on the sidewalk. Like the ailanthus (page 72) and the royal paulownia (pages 40 and 80), the white mulberry came to this country long before its invasive character was understood. Entrepreneurs began importing the tree as early as the seventeenth century with the hope of breeding silkworms and hatching an American silk industry. It is hard to picture now, but until the 1940s, when synthetic fibers began to replace silk, many towns, including some in upstate New York, based their economies on spinning silk. Attempts to foster a local silkworm-breeding industry failed but white mulberries spread rapidly and quickly supplanted the red. According to legend, this old specimen is the last of a group specifically planted for silkworm breeding. It was at the house just visible through its branches (though long before the tree itself was planted) that on September 11, 1776, John Adams, Benjamin Franklin, and Edward Rutledge met with Admiral Lord Richard Howe of the English navy for the failed "conference" at which the British hoped to end the American Revolution (see page 34). According to the historian David McCullough, the house had been "badly used by the Hessian Guard" and "looked no better than a stable." But "in a last-minute effort to decorate for the occasion—and dampen the smell—the floor had been spread with moss and green branches." After a cold meal and wine, the meeting began. "If America should fail," said Lord Howe, "I should feel and lament it like a brother." "My Lord," answered Franklin, "we will do our utmost endeavors to save your Lordship that mortification."

Copper or Purple Beech *Fagus sylvatica* 'Atropurpurea' 62"
Wave Hill, Riverdale, Bronx
April 23, 2010

Nobody who visits Wave Hill, the public garden and cultural center in Riverdale, can avoid the desire (though it should be resisted for the health of the tree) to push under the low-hanging boughs of the copper beech at the top of the Wave Hill House lawn and lean against the trunk gazing up into the gloom of the broad-spreading branches. At all hours of the day, in all seasons, with leaves or without, the shapely tree draws the eye, as if inviting some incomprehensible contact. In fact, the tree is in trouble. A natural mutation of the European beech on page 38, this tree shares with that one the disadvantage that it is growing in the United States. For reasons not fully understood, European beeches on this side of the Atlantic are more susceptible to the bleeding beech canker (*Phytoph-thora citricola*) and other diseases and don't live as long as those on their native soil. As a result, a specimen such as this one, just a little over a hundred years old, is already at the end of its life span here, though it would be just entering middle age overseas. From what we can tell, it was planted, along with four others of its kind, during the first decade of the twentieth century as part of a general makeover of Wave Hill by George W. Perkins, who had combined two adjoining properties to create the estate in 1903. A 1919 photograph shows one of those beeches as a sapling, and a 1939 map gives this one a diameter of 14 inches. Of the original five only three remain, and these are already showing signs of the canker that took off the other two (the one here has already lost a major limb since the photograph was taken). In response to the loss or eventual loss of its old trees, Wave Hill has begun planting replacement trees of species likely to withstand not only such diseases but also expected changes in the climate. In recent years, a Dutch elm disease–resistant elm and a cucumber magnolia have been put out at key spots, but not European beeches.

Silver Linden *Tilia tomentosa* 65.5"
Nethermead, Prospect Park, Brooklyn
October 15, 2009

"He remembered his grandfather," wrote Vladimir Nabokov in the first paragraph of the novel *Glory*, "...in one form and position: a corpulent old man, dressed completely in white, fair-whiskered, wearing a Panama hat and a piqué waiscoat rich in breloques (the most amusing of which was a dagger the size of a fingernail), sitting on a bench in front of the house in a linden's mobile shade." Introduced in 1767, the species is native to southeastern Europe and western Asia and is famous for its upright oval form in old age. It is also famous, as Nabokov indicates, for its shade. In the years before air-conditioning, the linden was an extremely popular shade tree and was planted in parks throughout New York City. (Two spots particularly effective in this regard, and famous in their own right for their trees, are the Linden Terrace in Fort Tryon Park in Manhattan and the pathways on the Greene and Tompkins Avenue sides of Herbert Von King Park in Brooklyn.) The lopsided appearance of this specimen on Prospect Park's Nethermead results from the loss of the second of its two forking central trunks in the early 1990s. The tree was already quite substantial on a 1935 map, with a diameter of 30 inches. I have photographed it in all weathers and remember particularly one brilliant fall afternoon an adolescent couple violently kissing beneath a nearby London plane. They had been going at it for some twenty minutes before they understood that my camera, aimed at the silver linden, might also be drawing them into its wide and permanent gaze. They didn't make a fuss—just moved around to the other side of the London plane—and eventually I moved on to another tree.

English Elm *Ulmus procera* 65"
Washington Square Park, Manhattan
November 18, 2011

Although Washington Square has not always been a park—it was the site of a cemetery, a parade ground, and private houses before the city named it a park in 1827—no major buildings have been erected on its 9.75 acres and, except for a few put up on the east side of the park by New York University, no tall buildings have been constructed around it. The only major structures built within the modern park were the fountain, completed in 1872, and the Washington Square Arch, constructed in 1890–92. Without basements to block roots, pavement to siphon off water, and surrounding rooftops to shade high branches, Washington Square is an ideal place for trees to grow, and the big English elm in the northwest corner has taken full advantage of this. Whether the tree is as old as legends claim is doubtful, but there is no question that it is the tallest of the English elms still growing in the city, and its trunk has the largest diameter. It harks back to a time when this part of Manhattan was outside city limits. Starting in the 1790s, the land on which it grows belonged to Thomas Ludlow, a downtown merchant who had apparently bought the property way up here beside the Minetta Brook to build a country house. Ludlow could very well have planted the tree along with others at the edge of his property near the corner of MacDougal Street (now Washington Square West) and Greenwich Lane (now straightened and called Washington Square North). Or somebody else could have planted it earlier: on a 1934 park map, the tree already had an estimated diameter of 48 inches. Historians have pretty much debunked the idea that the tree was used for hangings during the American Revolution, but popular culture keeps the notion alive. Such rumors were probably fueled by a misinterpretation of a detail in a letter by the Marquis de Lafayette, memories that sections of the park were once a burial ground, and a suggestive branch that once stretched out from the trunk to overhang the street. In part because of these myths, the so-called Hangman's Elm is today probably the best-known tree in Manhattan—though still, every day, hundreds of people walk by without looking up to notice it.

Snake Branch Spruce *Picea abies 'Virgata'* 23"
Benenson Ornamental Conifers, New York Botanical Garden, Bronx
May 5, 2009

If you take away the different institutions overseeing trees in New York City (the Parks Department, nonprofit garden and park groups, the cemeteries, private homeowners) and consider the trees as growing all basically in the same locality, New York City's urban forest becomes a different but no less magnificent mix. To think of such arboreal oddities as this snake branch spruce, for example, not in the specialized collection of conifers in the New York Botanical Garden to which it was transplanted in the 1940s, but in the workaday world of the pin oaks, Norway maples, and London planes outside the garden gates, is to see the trees not as rare objects but as the producers of oxygen, absorbers of carbon dioxide, and sources of food and shelter for animals that they are. It's hard to think that way, because to walk through the New York Botanical Garden on a rainy spring morning as the blossoms are coming out and beads of water are collecting on the grass is like walking through a painting or a dream, yet both the interior as well as the exterior of the garden are part of a larger ecosystem that makes equal use of all plants and is ruled over by a democracy of birds. As it turns out, by the volume of its boughs and the fact that those boughs stay green all winter, the snake branch spruce is an important player in this ecosystem. It grows here by an odd chance. Around a hundred years ago an accounting executive named Robert H. Montgomery, wanting to prolong his life by distracting himself from the cares of work, took up the hobby of collecting rare conifers from around the world and planting them on his hundred-acre estate in Cos Cob, Connecticut. In the 1940s he moved to Florida and gave the New York Botanical Garden two hundred specimens from his collection, of which this particular spruce—a cultivated variety of the Norway spruce, now about eighty years old—was one. Replanted in 1949 on fifteen acres along the Bronx River, this and the 199 specimens with it formed the basis for what has become, with some additions and replacements, one of the most unusual conifer gardens of the east coast.

Callery Pear *Pyrus calleryana* 14" (removed 2008)
Eleventh Avenue at 25th Street, Manhattan
April 24, 2002; November 14, 2002; February 7, 2003; April 19, 2003

In the Street Tree Census of 2006, the Callery pear was the second most widely planted street tree in Manhattan, following only the honeylocust. It was, and still is, prized for its fast growth, tolerance of pollution, and beauty in all four seasons. It can be found virtually everywhere, lighting up blocks with its white blossoms in the spring and glowing down avenues with its orange-yellow leaves in the fall. Brought into this country from China by way of France in the early twentieth century, the tree gained popularity as an urban street tree after the introduction of a hardy variety called Bradford in 1963. It was soon planted in virtually every city in the United States. My wife and I came upon this one in 2002 on our way to a gallery opening in Chelsea. I came back and photographed it many times and it became a sort of signature tree for me: people associated me with it and would tell me what they had seen when they passed it—whether a balloon was caught in its branches or somebody had left an umbrella leaning against the trunk or they had run into a friend on the block. A photographer friend sent me a print of a photograph he had taken of the tree from the roof-top of the building behind it. I lost my wallet while taking the winter shot; the next day a clerk from the post office called to say that somebody had found the wallet in the snow and put it into a mailbox. When I went to retrieve the wallet the cash was still inside. I made postcards of the tree and sent them around to friends and clients. It was not a big or unusual or important tree but it had a nice shape and went well with the building behind it and I liked it. It turned out to be the same species as a tree that had survived the collapse of the World Trade Center towers less than a year before, which the Parks Department was then nursing back to health with plans to replant it someday at ground zero. Today, the so-called Survivor Tree stands out as the only one of its species among the 412 swamp white oaks now growing at the 9/11 memorial site.

Site of the Callery Pear *Pyrus calleryana* 14"
Eleventh Avenue at 25th Street, Manhattan
April 24, 2008

One day in 2008 I drove by and the Callery pear was gone. The parking lot behind where it had grown had been turned into a construction site. A crane far taller than the missing tree cast an imperfect shadow on the building behind it. I e-mailed Fiona Watt, a former colleague at the Parks Department, and learned that the tree had been cut down to make way for the extension of the Number 7 subway line. Three Con Edison substations were to go there. The Metropolitan Transportation Authority had paid the city $22,500, or the equivalent of thirty new trees, for permission to cut this one down. "Not sure the fine really makes a difference," wrote Fiona, "although we did collect it." The city is full of stories like this. No crime has been committed, nobody has done anything quite wrong, but something that has existed in one place for a long time (or maybe even not a long time), something that has been an important part of that place for many people, is removed one day for totally unrelated reasons. I don't know that anything can be done about it. Maybe, in this case, somebody thought that so many Callery pears are planted in Manhattan (about 7,800 at last count) nobody would mind the loss of this one. Not until a couple of years after I took this picture, as I was beginning this book, did I realize that I had taken it on the very day, six years earlier, when I had shot the first picture of the tree. On that particular day, and on the days around it, the late afternoon sun funnels through a gap between two post office buildings and creates a spotlight effect on the sidewalk where the tree had grown. It was this effect, available for only those few days each year, that had caused the Callery pear to shine forth with such brilliance when my wife and I first noticed it.

Tree of Heaven *Ailanthus altissima* (not measured—removed 2002)
30th Street at Eleventh Avenue, Manhattan
May 28, 2002

As everyone knows, the tree of heaven is a weed tree, a vicious invasive that would take root in a soda can if given the opportunity. Just the sight of it, in many people's minds, breeds thoughts of insurrection against the urban grid. If you look closely at this specimen you will notice, aside from the domestic materials arranged alongside it, that somebody has attached a makeshift antenna to the railing of the abandoned railroad line above. Ailanthus was introduced to the United States from its native China as an ornamental tree in 1784 and quickly spread on its own. It is now the most common tree in New York, making up 9 percent of the urban forest. The specimen here grew in classic ailanthus territory, a seemingly forgotten spot beneath an abandoned railroad track. As is often the case with trees in New York City, when I returned eight months after taking the picture, the tree (or trees, as this actually seems to have been) was gone, along with the milk crates, the suitcase, and the cardboard box beneath it. The authorities, the cabinetmaker across the street suggested, had cut down the tree and hauled it away in an effort to "clean up the block." All that remained was the graffiti. I might have left it at that, but as time went on more facts emerged. It turned out that the cabinetmaker didn't have the full story. In March 2002, two months before I took the picture, the city council had passed a resolution advocating the renovation of the "abandoned railroad track" as a walking trail. A public-private partnership was to clear the tracks and transform them into the elevated park now known as the High Line. The ailanthus had been cut down during the initial clearing stage. As time went on, sophisticated plantings began to re-create the look of the tracks during their years of abandonment. The gardeners, however, avoided reintroducing the non-native ailanthus. Wanting to maintain the spontaneous feel of the abandoned tracks, they planted the similarly leaved native sumac instead.

Honeylocust *Gleditsia triacanthos* 6.5"
Horace Harding Boulevard, Elmhurst, Queens
November 4, 2002

This small honeylocust beside an overpass of the Long Island Expressway is not on any official lists, is not watched over by community group or concerned citizen or botanical garden, and is not anything at all really but a small honeylocust that might or might not make it through the next decade, beside a footpath that leads from the Queens Center Mall under the expressway to Rego Park. It was sunlight, coming through the clouds after a rainstorm and happening to hit the tree in this way, that caused me to photograph it. Popular for its hardiness and its slender, graceful appearance, which is unlike that of most other such trees in this country, the native species is the most-planted street tree in Manhattan and the Bronx but the fifth most planted in Queens, after the Norway maple, London plane, pin oak, and Callery pear. Overall, it makes up 2.3 percent of New York's urban forest. Honeylocusts traditionally had thorns, which are thought to have evolved to protect them from predators. Nearly all honeylocusts planted today are a thornless variety known as *forma inermis.* As children in Pierrepont Playground in Brooklyn Heights, Rolf Hamburger, Shep Faison, Peter Heller, and I advanced on one another with the rattling brown seed pods, which made excellent, if dull, swords. The sweet pulp inside the long, curving, very hard pods gives the tree its name. Although I took this photograph at a slow shutter speed, a passerby on his way to Rego Park managed to leave his sneaker and part of his leg in the frame. The neighborhood of Rego Park got its name from a commercial organization, the Real Good Construction Company, which built 525 eight-room houses on farmland to create an instant community in the 1920s. Forty years later, Samuel J. LeFrak constructed LeFrak City in a forty-two-acre swamp nearby. When completed in 1966, his five-thousand-unit co-op complex consisted of twenty sixteen-story residential buildings, two office towers, and its own post office, bank, supermarkets, and branch of the Queens public library. Thus Queens was developed and a rural landscape transformed to an urban one.

Southern Magnolia *Magnolia grandiflora* 20"
679 Lafayette Avenue, Bedford-Stuyvesant, Brooklyn
June 3, 2010

This slow-growing evergreen with its big, shiny leaves and large loose lemon-scented flowers has been growing on this block since around 1885, when a liquor merchant, William Lemken, had it shipped to Brooklyn from North Carolina and planted in front of his new brownstone (the smaller tree beside it was planted later). A stock tree of southern plantations still considered unsuitable for planting this far north, the tree managed to survive more than half a century of Brooklyn winters by, in effect, hugging the warm buildings behind it before a developer began eyeing the block for an urban renewal project in the 1960s. It was then that Hattie Carthan, a community activist with an interest in trees, created a campaign to save the tree. Mrs. Carthan raised $7,000 through local schools to build a masonry wall behind the tree to protect it from the wind (the wall now carries the mural of Mrs. Carthan), and she and other neighbors applied to the New York City Landmarks Preservation Commission and succeeded in having the tree designated an official city landmark in 1970—one of only two individual trees in the city ever designated as a landmark and the only one still alive (see page 20). After saving the tree and buildings, Mrs. Carthan went on to found the Bedford-Stuyvesant Neighborhood Tree Corps, a precursor to the citywide group the Green Guerillas that involved children in tree care. As chairwoman of the Bedford-Stuyvesant Beautification Committee, Mrs. Carthan brought together block associations to plant more than 1,500 trees throughout the neighborhood. She created the nonprofit Magnolia Tree Earth Center in the brownstones behind the tree, and after her death in 1984 the Magnolia Tree Earth Center and other community organizations continued to use the brownstones for offices. The Parks Department commissioner Henry J. Stern named a community garden a few blocks away for Mrs. Carthan in 1998. The tree is across the street from Herbert Von King Park, one of the oldest parks in Brooklyn, established in 1857 and designed by Frederick Law Olmsted and Calvert Vaux in 1871.

English Elm *Ulmus procera* 58"

St. Nicholas Avenue at 163rd Street, Manhattan
July 31, 2009

Although it is clear that English elms were especially popular at the end of the eighteenth and beginning of the nineteenth centuries, only when they die can we learn, from the rings, when they actually went into the ground. For a long time historians thought that Colonel Roger Morris planted this one around 1765 during the construction of his Palladian-style summer house just a few blocks southeast (the house, known as the Morris-Jumel Mansion, can be visited today). The tree would have been planted, along with several others, along the Boston Post Road, now St. Nicholas Avenue, which ran through the 130-acre property. If this were correct the tree, then very small, would have been growing here in 1776, when George Washington made his headquarters at the Morris house after the Battle of Long Island. By then the Morris family, who were loyalists, had fled to England, and their exquisite house with its two-story columned portico, its octagonal drawing room, and its strategic views in all directions had become the favorite living quarters not only of Washington but, later, of Lieutenant General Sir Henry Clinton of the British army and the Hessian commander Baron Wilhelm von Knyphausen. As recounted by the historian David McCullough, during his thirty-seven days here Washington revived the morale of his army with a victory at Harlem Heights, watched as fires destroyed much of Manhattan to the south, endured the hanging of the Connecticut schoolmaster Nathan Hale as a spy, observed the breaching of American defenses at Forts Lee and Washington, and issued the order for the army to move to White Plains. Why his soldiers, and later the English, desperate for firewood, would have left this tree standing and burned most others in the vicinity is worth asking. How it has managed to survive from Washington's day until ours in such an increasingly cramped position is a mystery that the Parks Department is anxious not so much to solve as to replicate. The department has taken cuttings from the tree and cloned them in an attempt to reproduce the tree's success elsewhere in the city.

Royal Paulownia *Paulownia tomentosa* 7.5" (removed 2006)
Post Road Plaza, Pelham Manor, Westchester County
May 8, 2002

In this once desolate spot near the intersection of the Albany and Boston Post Roads, just over the Bronx line in Pelham Manor, the most prominent feature of the landscape, visible for miles around, like the billboard of Dr. T. J. Eckleburg in *The Great Gatsby*, is this arching metal framework built to carry a fuel pipe over Eastchester Creek. In other parts of the city where fuel transport and processing facilities are more common, such a structure would probably not stand out so dramatically, but here, in this low-rise neighborhood, a thing of such height and geometric majesty dominates the view. The royal paulownia I found growing beneath it in 2002 seems to have seeded itself, not surprising given the tenacious growing power of this nonnative species (see page 40), but uncannily perfect placement nevertheless by whatever bird or rodent or current of wind or water happened to drop the seed in this precise spot. Even less surprising, perhaps, is that the tree is no longer there. A few years after I took the picture, a cleanup of the Post Road Plaza brought a Fairway supermarket and "75,000 square feet of gastronomical greatness" to a place once dominated by chain-link fences, cracked parking lots, abandoned shopping plazas, chop shops, and this tree. As part of this sprucing up, the owners of the Post Road Plaza lovingly repaved the parking lot down to the water's edge and removed the tree. More a brook at this point in its passage to the Long Island Sound, Eastchester Creek becomes the Hutchinson River when it enters the Bronx just south of here. The river is named for Anne Hutchinson, the midwife who was expelled from Boston in 1637 for her dangerously popular criticisms of the prevailing Puritan dogma. After a stint in Providence she settled by the mouth of the river where it enters Eastchester Bay and began building a farm. She and most of her children and followers were murdered by the local Siwanoy in 1643. It's sometimes hard to remember how scary things were back then when forests still covered the land and fearful things happened to people outside the city walls.

Cedar of Lebanon *Cedrus libani* 100.5"
Weeping Beech Park, Flushing, Queens
July 28, 2010

Before the chain-link fence, before the iron fence, before the park benches, before the comfort station—before the playground itself, when fields stretched away on either side and Flushing was a village still known for its trees—a local nursery-man planted this cedar near the house of his great-grandparents. Native to a small strip of western Asia that includes modern-day Lebanon, Syria, and southwestern Turkey, and first brought to this continent during colonial times, cedars of Lebanon have been admired through the ages for their graceful broad-spreading branches and flat-topped crowns and had graced the estates of wealthy Europeans long before they arrived here. Old photographs depict several thriving in Flushing during the late nineteenth and early twentieth centuries—one in the front yard of the former home of William Prince, the last owner of the oldest nursery in Flushing—but the forces of urbanization seem to have taken their toll on those long ago, and as far as we know this specimen in Weeping Beech Park, planted by Robert Bowne Parsons in the 1890s, is the only large one remaining in Flushing. It is in fact young for its kind: trees estimated to be as old as two thousand years still grow in protected groves in Lebanon. But it was one of the northernmost true Lebanon cedars planted in North America before global warming began changing growing conditions. Whether Parsons planted it temporarily, as nursery stock during the declining years of his family's nursery business, or permanently to grace the streetscape of Flushing is one of the mysteries that still surround it. On the afternoon I photographed it, a group of young men watched me from a cement table in the playground, where they were playing dominoes. "I used to climb that tree," one of them said. "All the way to the top there. All the way to the top I'd be, looking down on everybody." As I packed up my camera, the clacking of the dominoes and the low voices of the young men continued in the dusk, and continued in my mind long after I had left the park.

Dawn Redwoods *Metasequoia glyptostroboides* 23.5", 29"
Benenson Ornamental Conifers, New York Botanical Garden, Bronx
May 14, 2009; January 5, 2010

In 1943 Chan Wang, a forester from the Ministry of Agriculture and Forests in Chongqing, China, visited a remote region of Sichuan on a routine forest inspection. On his way, he stopped to see an old college friend who was principal of an agricultural high school. The friend told him about a strange tree growing in a remote village, a deciduous conifer that he could not identify. Intrigued, Wang changed his route, went to the village, and for three days collected specimens of the tree, then continued on his way. Later, he identified the specimens as belonging to *Glyptostrobus pensilis*, a deciduous conifer common in China. Two years afterward, however, Wang gave some of the samples to an assistant teacher at the National Central University in Chongqing, and the teacher brought them to Wan-Chun Cheng, a dendrology professor at the university. Professor Cheng realized right away that Wang's conclusion had been wrong and that the strange tree had not yet been identified in China and was quite possibly a new species or even genus. He arranged for a graduate student to go back to the village for more samples and, after studying these, sent some to Hsen-Hsu Hu, director of a biology institute in Beijing. Professor Hu agreed immediately that the samples were a new find, but he soon realized that they matched a genus previously published by a Japanese researcher, Shigero Miki, in 1941. Miki had proposed the genus *Metasequoia* based on fossils of a prehistoric deciduous redwood that had flourished in Japan and other parts of the world, including the United States, until about 23 million years ago. As far as he or anyone else knew the genus had vanished from the earth as a living thing sometime during the Miocene epoch. The discovery of a living relic caused a worldwide stir. Professors Cheng and Hu corresponded with dendrologists in Europe and the United States, including Elmer D. Merrill at Harvard's Arnold Arboretum and Ralph W. Chaney in Berkeley. Drs. Merrill and Chaney mailed

Professor Cheng money for seed collection. Professor Cheng sent an assistant out into the countryside to fulfill the request. This time, the assistant not only collected seeds from the original tree but, following the directions of local residents, found a valley where more than one hundred of the trees were growing wild. Drs. Cheng and Hu sent packets of seeds to Drs. Merrill and Chaney and others. In 1948 Dr. Merrill forwarded a packet from one of these shipments to the New York Botanical Garden. Two years later, Chinese botanists sent a second packet. The New York Botanical Garden planted seeds from both packets on its grounds in 1950. The trees in the Metasequoia Grove in the Benenson Ornamental Conifers section, some of them now reaching heights of nearly a hundred feet, come from those original seeds. Today, *Metasequoia* are being planted along streets and in backyards around the world. (In New York City, beautiful examples can be seen in the Brooklyn Botanic Garden and at the Liz Christy Community Garden on Houston Street in Manhattan.) But few groves outside China have reached the proportions of this one at the New York Botanical Garden. Whether dense with foliage on a rainy summer morning or bare and tall in the low sun of a winter afternoon, the trees draw the eye in all seasons.

American Elm *Ulmus americana* 59"

Central Park, East Meadow near East 97th Street, Manhattan
February 26, 2010

In a rare and unusual book, published in 1890, called *Typical Elms and Other Trees of Massachusetts*, with a preface by Oliver Wendell Holmes Jr., L. L. Dame and Henry Brooks argue that American elms divide themselves into three physical types: the *Vase*, the *Weeping-Willow*, and the *Oak-Tree*. Among the American elms still growing in New York City, this one on the East Meadow would seem to fit the *Oak-Tree* type (here described in comparison to the *Vase*): "ramification usually takes place within ten or fifteen feet of the ground; the long curves give way to straight lines and abrupt turns; the regular arches disappear, grace and symmetry being transmuted, as it were, in the alembic of Nature, into sturdiness and strength." The elm on Ridge Boulevard in Bay Ridge, Brooklyn (page 52), would seem to fit the *Vase* type, and the elm across from the Museum of Natural History at 77th Street and Central Park West in Manhattan (page 94) the *Weeping-Willow*. One of the original specimen trees planted by Frederick Law Olmsted and Calvert Vaux during the construction of the park in the mid-nineteenth century, this one is the focal point of the East Meadow, an open grassy area that Olmsted originally conceived of as an arboretum of American trees. "When you get years of good fall color," said Neil Calvanese, Central Park's vice president for operations, "this tree lights up that whole south side in yellow. It dominates the whole south vista." Calvanese and his staff check the tree for signs of Dutch elm disease every week during the summer. The fungus has been found in other trees not far away. The tree author Ned Barnard once told me that when he looks at this tree he is always reminded that the trees in Central Park have now "reached sizes that Olmsted never knew and never saw." I think of this elm in relation to the osage orange Olmsted planted at his house on Staten Island (see page 24) and the horsechestnuts he placed around Fort Greene Park in Brooklyn. These are trees that have taken on lives far beyond what their planter could have foreseen, yet which, still growing in the places he put them, seem, as a living group, to shape his ongoing presence in the city.

Eastern Cottonwood *Populus deltoides* 73"

184 Sprague Avenue at George Street, Tottenville, Staten Island
March 10, 2006

Cottonwoods are not especially long-lived trees and foresters tend to deride them for their soft wood and weak limbs. "A messy tree often dropping leaves, flowers, fruits, twigs and branches," writes the horticulturist Michael A. Dirr. "Impressive in river bottoms and should remain there." Nevertheless, even more than the now endangered American elm, cottonwoods are fast growers and have been valued by many for how impressive they look when they get big. This one in suburban Tottenville at the southern end of Staten Island has gone well beyond its expected life span as the commuity has changed around it. When I first photographed it in 1998 a different house stood beneath it. The owner of the house, Frank Supina, came out and posed for a photograph under the tree and told me that he had lived in the house for fifty-three years. When I came back to photograph the tree again in 2006, both Mr. Supina and his house were gone. Two new houses had been put up in place of the old one. Three pines climbed up the side of one of the new ones exactly as they had up the side of the old one. It turned out that Frank Supina's son, Bob, lived in a still-intact older house directly behind the two new ones. Bob Supina told me that his family had decided to sell his father's house after his father died on January 1, 2005, and that the new owner had subdivided the property and sold it as two lots. Such diminution of acreage is not unusual for Tottenville: up the hill on Prospect Avenue, Bob Supina said, twenty new houses had recently been built on a property formerly belonging to one. He said that he himself had lived in Tottenville his entire life. He had moved to the house under the cottonwood when he was five. He worked in electrical construction but retired in 2003. He enjoyed going into Manhattan from time to time and had recently been to see *Jersey Boys*. "A great play," he said. As we spoke he kept glancing up at the tree above us. It semed to connect us not only to each other but to his father, to the missing house, and to the neighborhood as it was now and had been during his life.

Tanyosho Pine *Pinus densiflora 'Umbraculiferas'* 24"
Ross Conifer Arboretum, New York Botanical Garden, Bronx
May 5, 2009

The four tanyosho pines growing across from the reflecting pool near the Conservatory Gate at the New York Botanical Garden are what is left of an original grove of six planted in 1908. Pines like these have been cultivated in Japan for centuries to highlight the intense color of the bark and the flat, layered way the branches spread out. One of the traditional goals of Japanese gardeners was to create small spaces that would give the effect of larger or different ones. Because they were planted so close together so long ago, the four tanyosho pines have grown in tandem as if they were a single plant, each one dependent on the others to block wind and limit the sway of branches. Fallen needles around the trunks have decayed into a loamy layer that matches the color of the bark and also fertilizes the trees. As the branches have risen and spread a clear space has opened beneath in which trunks and limbs seem like supporting structures of a soft red room. The tanyosho form their own system within the larger framework of the garden's conifer arboretum, which itself contains many other trees with similarly unusual and alluring qualities. Spiraling out from the Victorian glass Conservatory, the conifer collection was one of the first arrangements of trees put in the ground after the garden opened in 1896. At that time, all of the trees except those in the fifty-acre forest were arranged according to their evolutionary relationships: pines with pines, oaks with oaks, maples with maples. This was thought to be the most educational, rational way to organize species. Whether a tree was a pure specimen as it would have been found in the wild or, like the tanyosho pines, a cultivated variety selected for a special trait mattered less than that it be in the same genus as its neighbor. Horticulturists now often experiment with different arrangements, but with their intense concentrations of similar plants the older collections retain a kind of breathtaking simplicity and integrity.

American Elm *Ulmus americana* 41"
Central Park West at 77th Street, Manhattan
September 24, 2007

When the Central Park Conservancy began managing the park in 1980, Dutch elm disease was rampant, killing more than a hundred American elms a year. The conservancy instituted a program that foresters call "sanitation," in which diseased branches were immediately removed before the fungus could spread to the rest of a tree, and the entire tree removed if the fungus managed to spread anyway. As a precaution, the conservancy also injected trees with fungicide—especially those near an already-infected elm—but the main focus was quick removal of the infected branch or tree. The result was a reduction in the number of elms that succumbed to the disease to fewer than twenty a year, and sometimes as few as ten. Since, at last count, the park contained 1,643 elms (both English and American), loss at this rate suggests that the park could retain a selection of older elms for another eighty years, by which point new disease-resistant cultivars now being introduced will have had a chance to reach some level of maturity. This hundred-year-old specimen by the Naturalists Gate, across the street from the Museum of Natural History, is sometimes called the Humboldt elm because the bronze bust of the German scientist Alexander von Humboldt (1769–1859) rests on a pedestal just south of the tree (outside the frame of the picture). Humboldt was a scientist whose attempts to integrate huge amounts of knowledge into a single book, based on his own explorations in South America and Siberia and discoveries at home in Germany, led to the five-volume *Kosmos*, published in 1845. The book was important not only to Charles Darwin but also to Edgar Allan Poe, who dedicated his prose poem *Eureka* to Humboldt in 1848. Lawyers might call the upended paving blocks around the base of the Humboldt elm a trip hazard, but to Humboldt himself they might represent the healthy urge of a tree to fight for water and nutrients against the human desire for smoothness and order.

European Hornbeam *Carpinus betulus 'Fastigiata'* 27"
New York Botanical Garden, Bronx
May 5, 2009

Sometimes—and often, as with people, simply because of the way they appear on a particular day, in some combination of weather and light—a tree stands out not for its age or its size or the unusualness of its species but for the perfection of its form. There are trees that can only be called good-looking. This (for me at least) is the case with the New York Botanical Garden's Fastigiate European hornbeam, a fairly ordinary, popular variety of nonnative hornbeam cultivated for the upright growing habit of its multiple branches, which fan outward without a main trunk sometimes as high as 40 feet. Although a few years older than I (born in 1959), the New York Botanical Garden specimen is not old in arboreal terms (it was purchased in 1957 from Hicks Nursery in Long Island) and exhibits none of the scaling bark, dying branches, or other characteristics of compromised trees. It is simply, purely, what it is supposed to be. Like that of the American hornbeam in Prospect Park (see page 56), the wood of European hornbeam is extremely hard and strong. The species is susceptible to few insects and diseases, and it is likely that this one, always under the care of gardeners at the New York Botanical Garden, will continue to mature slowly in its characteristic way for many years to come. Because of its orderly, wide-spreading branches, European hornbeam has long been a favored tree for hedges, especially in England. In New York City, three hornbeam hedges create a mazelike entrance to the aquatic garden at Wave Hill in the Bronx.

Chinese Maidenhair *Ginkgo biloba* 57"
Isham Park, Inwood, Manhattan
November 17, 2011

Like the dawn redwood and the osage orange (see pages 84 and 114), the ginkgo is an evolutionary oddity, an ancient type of tree that seemed to be dying out of the world and should have gone extinct but did not. Human cultivation of ginkgoes around temples in China and later in Japan kept them in circulation when their natural spread—once worldwide—had been reduced to a few wild plants in isolated parts of China. In the United States, the species was first imported and planted for specimen trees, meant to grace an estate or city park. Later, taking advantage of their hardiness across planting zones and in poor conditions, cities began to plant them on streets (building superintendents love them because in the fall their leaves drop all at once, making cleanup easier). In 2005, ginkgoes accounted for 10 percent of the street trees in Manhattan. The unusually large specimen in the southeast corner of Isham Park was probably planted in the late 1860s or early 1870s at the entrance of the carriage road to the estate of William B. Isham, a successful tanner whose property became Isham Park in 1927. A 1925 photograph shows the stately tree towering over the caretaker's cottage that then stood behind it. On a 1934 map the tree had a diameter of 36 inches. It is now one of the largest of its species in the city. Many generations of Inwood residents have passed under its broad-spreading, delicate branches. In the retaining wall beneath and just to the left of the tree (not shown) is one of the original eighteenth-century milestones from when this stretch of Broadway was the Boston Post Road and formed the main route out of Manhattan, across the King's Bridge to the mainland and eventually to Boston. The marker was part of a series erected under the direction of Benjamin Franklin and indicated 12 miles from (or to) City Hall.

English Elm *Ulmus procera* 63.5"

Central Park at East 90th Street, Manhattan
February 26, 2010

Numerous outstanding trees never made it onto the city's Great Trees list in 1985, often for no better reason than that too many other trees of the same species or from the same geographical area had already been chosen. Trees had to be nominated by community groups, and not all of the community groups were aware of all of the trees. Although not on that original list, this one deserves inclusion not only for its commanding position at the grand entrance to Central Park at 90th Street and Fifth Avenue—officially called the Engineers' Gate but commonly known as the Runners' Gate—but also for its species and size. It is one of the last standing healthy English elms, and it is a big one. Although presumably younger than the specimen in the northwest corner of Washington Square Park (page 64), it is only two inches narrower in trunk diameter. As is common with older English elms, this one is particularly prone to putting forth secondary shoots from its branches, giving it a hairy appearance. Despite the messy look, foresters are reluctant to remove the shoots, which seem to help the older elms maintain an adequate level of photosynthesis. In an effort to prolong its life, the Central Park Conservancy has fenced off a considerable area beneath it to create a planting bed. It was originally planted among layers of rubble that would have been put down when the park was built, and the roots have grown out into the spaces among the rubble. Saturdays at dawn, bicyclists zoom past the tree in packs as part of Century Road Club Association races, and each year on the first Sunday in November exhausted runners barely give it a glance as they enter Central Park for the last two miles of the New York City Marathon. The tree stands at the starting point for the multikilometer running races sponsored by the New York Road Runners Club and at the entrances to the Bridle Path and reservoir tracks, two other important routes for runners.

American Elm *Ulmus americana* 39.5"
Harlem River Drive, Manhattan
October 10, 2003

American elms have the capacity to bend in all kinds of ways to accommodate obstructions. In this case, the obstruction is the steep, thickly wooded hillside of Highbridge Park, to the right of the tree outside the frame of the picture. In comparison, the open sky over the Harlem River Drive seems to have been an attractive alternative. The tree was probably planted in 1934 as part of a general revamping of this stretch of the drive, then known as the Speedway, under the Parks Department commissioner Robert Moses. On the park map from that year, a row of newly planted 3-inch elms forms a tiny allee with a row of newly planted 3-inch maples along the western side of the Speedway. Sworn in the year before, Moses had greatly expanded the workforce of the Parks Department and undertaken a major series of projects in all five boroughs, among them the upgrade to the Speedway. The Speedway originally opened in 1898 and was for many years a fashionable carriage drive. Automobiles began using it in 1919 and it was paved in 1922. Starting in the 1940s, Moses began rebuilding it as a connecting route between the Triborough and George Washington bridges, and it reopened as the Harlem River Drive in 1964. The bridge behind the tree, called the Highbridge, was completed in 1848 and carried water from the Croton Aqueduct across the Harlem River to reservoirs in Manhattan and thence to the sinks and bathtubs of Manhattan residents. Until the advent of electric pumps, gravity-induced pressure in the system was sufficient only to bring water to buildings of six or fewer floors. The completion of the New Croton Aqueduct in 1917 ended the use of the Highbridge to carry water, but not to carry pedestrians, which continued until 1970. It is the oldest bridge, and the only one exclusively for pedestrians, connecting Manhattan to the mainland. Among residents who made use of it when it opened was Edgar Allan Poe, who spent much of the last melancholy year of his life strolling across it from his cottage on Kingsbridge Road. A plan to reopen it to walkers and bicyclists has been in the works since 2000 and is scheduled to be completed in 2013.

American Sycamore *Platanus occidentalis* 62"
Alice Austen House, Clifton, Staten Island
July 30, 2009

The tree is hollow. Not only is it hollow but the inside is charred and blackened as if burned out and cauterized. Not only is the inside charred and blackened but the trunk has begun to grow back around its own hollow, blackened interior, so that before long, if the tree is left alone, the trunk may try to surround and cover its own hollowness. Evidently a bolt of lightning struck the tree and split part of it off and hollowed out the rest, and the reason it assumes this awkward shape, so thick at the base and so one-sidedly narrow at the top, is because of that catastrophic event in its past. I have not yet met anyone who remembers that event, so it must have happened some time ago. I have not met anyone who knows anything about the tree, aside from the fact that it is associated with the photographer Alice Austen, who lived in the Carpenter Gothic cottage behind it. Abandoned by her father before she was born, raised by her mother in the cottage, which belonged to her grandparents, and taking her maternal grandfather's name, Alice Austen first began to take pictures in 1876, at the age of ten, when her uncle, a ship captain, brought a dry plate camera back from England and let her try it. Within a few years she had become, without knowing it, one of the most accomplished photographers in New York. An amateur who photographed her family, friends, house, social activities, and travels, she ended up creating, purely for her own pleasure, an archive of the life of nineteenth-century upper-class New Yorkers that is one of the best on record. In 1950 a photo researcher discovered 3,500 of her glass-plate negatives in the basement of the Staten Island Historical Society. Curious, the researcher made inquiries about the photographer and discovered that Alice Austen was still alive. She had lost her grandfather's house and was living in a poorhouse. Moved to a private nursing home in 1951, Austen died in 1952. Since then her work has gained increasing recognition, and her house is now a museum. The tree continues to grow out back.

Tuliptree *Liriodendron tulipfera* 76"
Alley Pond Park, Queens
November 4, 2005

By height and diameter this is the biggest tree in Queens. One of the pleasures of visiting it is to discover that it is not an isolated so-called Great Tree but one of several especially tall specimens in a miraculously intact stand of mature forest in a hollow beside the Long Island Expressway. So close does it grow to the six lanes of traffic that you can spot it as you drive by on the westbound side of the highway. Even when you sit down next to it, roughly in the spot from which this picture was taken, the sounds of cars and trucks pretty much drown out those of the birds and insects. People often compare this tree to the very large tuliptree in Clove Lakes Park on Staten Island (see page 108). That tree is also the biggest in its borough, and speculation about the relative ages of these two continues. I showed pictures of both to Neil Pederson, the dendrochronologist from the Tree-Ring Lab at Columbia University's Lamont-Doherty Earth Observatory who cored the post oaks on page 118. From the balding bark and narrow, dense crown, Dr. Pederson guessed that this one was older, despite its smaller diameter. Especially in trees older than one hundred years, diameter bears little relation to age and other factors become more important. From tree rings in the Hudson Valley going back five hundred years, Dr. Pederson has discovered that the past hundred years were the rainiest in five centuries. The past forty were wetter still and, since 2003, annual precipitation has grown even more. What this means is that younger trees in the Hudson Valley have benefited from better conditions at an early age than older ones have and would tend to have grown bigger faster. On a park map of 1943, this tree had an estimated diameter of 48 inches. When I photographed it in 2005, the diameter was 76 inches. If that earlier figure is to be believed, its girth had grown 28 inches in sixty-two years. If the tree had grown at that same rate since it sprouted it would be 168 years old. But given the varying conditions over the past two centuries, not only of rainfall but of temperature and shade, the chances that it grew at that same rate since it sprouted are pretty much nil.

Tuliptree *Liriodendron tulipfera* 87"

Clove Lakes Park, Staten Island

July 30, 2009

When the city developed Clove Lakes Park in the 1930s, the section where this tuliptree grows contained a two-story house in the path of a proposed railway tunnel. The tunnel was never built, and the house was dismantled and carted away to make way for the park. Apparently distracted by the necessity of documenting the house and railway tunnel, however, the engineers in charge of making a map of the property at that time apparently failed to record this tuliptree. Many other tulips, oaks, maples, and other species are included on the map, but none seems large enough or in a reasonable enough spot to account for the huge tuliptree growing there today, which has the largest diameter of any single-trunked tree I have measured in the city. Extravagant claims are often made about the age of this tree. An optimistic estimate comes from a neighboring specimen—perhaps an offspring of this one—that the Parks Department was forced to cut down in 2008 after it was struck by lightning. The smaller tree had a diameter of 52.5 inches and an informal count of the rings dated it to 154 years. Extrapolating from this information, and assuming the same growth rate, the parent tree, with a diameter of 87 inches, would have been 256 years old on the day I photographed it in 2009. But as Ed Cook, the director of Columbia University's Tree-Ring Lab, explained, "Large trees growing in the open may look old, but tend to grow fast and are not as old as they seem to be"; furthermore, Neil Pederson, also of the Tree-Ring Lab, guessed from pictures that this tuliptree was probably younger than the one in Alley Pond Park (see page 106). As mentioned elsewhere (page 48), early settlers and Native Americans called the trees "canoe wood" because, when hollowed out, their broad, straight trunks made excellent, if tippy, boats. The "tulip" refers to the shape of the orange-yellow flowers that bloom in May. Tuliptrees are among the tallest trees on the east coast, and the lovely blossoms often go unnoticed. Far above the heads of unsuspecting humans they put on a private show for the hummingbirds, dragonflies, butterflies, and bees that know where to look for the succulent nectar.

European Beeches *Fagus sylvatica* 'Laciniata' and 'Quercifolia'

Kissena Park Historic Grove, Flushing, Queens

May 21, 2009

At any time during daylight hours, and even after daylight has gone, throughout the year, Flushing residents can be found hitting tennis balls to each other across the dozen or so courts 300 feet west of these beeches. Tennis has been played in Kissena Park since the 1930s. Visiting the park on a warm spring evening, hearing the constant *thwock* of the balls against the freshly painted concrete courts, it seems as if it might have been played here forever. But Kissena Park, which also contains a boating pond and a bicycle racing track, is famous less for its recreational than for its botanical heritage. It was here, in 1839, that an itinerant Quaker preacher named Samuel Bowne Parsons opened a nursery that, in the hands of his sons, Samuel Parsons Jr. and Robert Bowne Parsons, came to cover much of the land in Flushing. The nursery supplied trees to Frederick Law Olmsted and Calvert Vaux for both Central Park and Prospect Park and introduced numerous exotic species to the United States, including Japanese maple, weeping beech (page 20), flowering dogwood, and (for better or worse) white mulberry (pages 58, 126). Samuel Parsons Jr. later became a well-known landscape architect, the partner of Vaux and superintendent of planting in Central Park. When his father, the founder of the business, died in 1906, the family sold a section of the nurseries to the city for Kissena Park. Seventy-five years later, in 1981, a Parks Department horticulturist, Shelly Stiles, was sent to clean up a messy fourteen-acre section of the park and discovered the massive and unusual specimens still growing in their original rows.

White Pine Grove *Pinus strobus*
Arthur Ross Pinetum, Central Park, Manhattan
October 12, 2000

Conspicuously absent from New York City's streets are white pines, which arborists consider impractical to plant along sidewalks because they are vulnerable to pollution and road salt, don't like the alkalinity of city soils, and grow too large. For a long time, pines were also absent from Central Park. During the original construction of the park from 1857–73, the park's architects, Frederick Law Olmsted and Calvert Vaux, had planted many types of pines, especially along the West Drive, which was known as the Winter Drive because of its evergreens. But during much of the first half of the twentieth century a planting policy dictated the replacement of dead conifers with deciduous species, and by the late 1960s pines were nearly absent from the park. Yet pines, particularly white pines, were an important feature of the native forest of Manhattan, and their absence seemed unnatural and even a sign of the park's decline. In the early 1970s the philanthropist Arthur Ross, whose background in the paper industry gave him a particular interest in pines, proposed planting a screen of white pines at the northern end of the Great Lawn to hide the bare brick backs of the police precinct and a maintenance building. Working with Cornelius O'Shea, a horticulturist at the Parks Department, and Henry Hope Reed, curator of Central Park, Mr. Ross ended up planting something far more elaborate than a screen. He created one of the very first and still one of the only pinetums in a public park, a swirling swath of evergreens that now stretches from the east to the west drives and across the northern end of the Great Lawn, and includes not only native white pines but Himalayan white pines, Japanese red pines, Australian pines, Swiss stone pines, Virginia scrub pines, pitch pines, a laceback pine, and more. An evolving collection, which the Central Park Conservancy has continued to augment since Mr. Ross's death in 2007, the Pinetum not only revives the historical place of pines in the park but honors a mission of Olmsted and Vaux to create an arboretum to educate the public about trees.

Osage Orange Grove *Maclura pomifera*
Crocheron Park, Bayside, Queens
April 21, 2010

There is a hypothesis that the 5-inch-diameter green fruit balls dropped by osage orange trees were eaten and dispersed by wild horses and mastodons during the Pleistocene epoch, and that the reduction in growing area of this unique tree, which once covered the continent, to a single valley near the intersections of Texas, Oklahoma, and Arkansas was caused by the extinction of those seed-dispersing creatures at the end of the Pleistocene, or about 12,000 years ago. Few animals today, including humans, can eat the foul-tasting fruit, which exists, as one writer put it, as a kind of ecological "anachronism" in the twenty-first century. The current spread of the trees outside the Red River Valley, to which they were confined when Europeans arrived, results from humans acting as redispersing agents. Native Americans used the supple wood to make bows, and a particular tribe is thought to have enjoyed a virtual monopoly in trading it far and wide. Settlers used it for different purposes. When grown together in a row, the scraggly, thorny trees made excellent fences for livestock, hedges, and screens. To this day, without necessarily knowing why, people in the Midwest sometimes refer to osage oranges as "hedge apples." During the nineteenth century, east coast landscape gardeners, including Frederick Law Olmsted (see page 24), began experimenting with osage oranges both ornamentally and as hedgerows. It was probably this second use, as a barrier, that led to the planting of more than a hundred in a T shape between two properties in Bayside sometime in the late nineteenth century. Subsequently acquired by the city and named Golden and Crocheron Parks, after the families that had previously owned them, the properties are now known more for their tennis courts, baseball fields, dog runs, and views of Littleneck Bay than for their unusual collection of osage oranges. In 2010 seventy-six of the original trees remained, many fallen and bent, with poison ivy and weeds creeping among them. The wood is exceptionally hardy and rot resistant but some have begun to succumb to old age and overcompetition, and I wonder what their future will be.

Black Tupelo *Nyssa sylvatica*
The Ramble, Central Park
October 20, 2010

In an attempt to keep the soil around trees loose and well fertilized, the Central Park Conservancy often carefully breaks up the ground, spreads wood chips, and installs fences around the bases to protect roots from soil compaction. Few trees in the park, however, have had the chance to benefit so fully from this kind of care as the black tupelo in the Ramble. Like a witness in a government protection program the tree, once prominently visible, has been carefully hidden in plain sight, at the edge of the clearing where it has grown for as long as anyone can remember. If only every tree could receive such treatment! When I first saw it in 1996, heavily trodden dirt surrounded it, open space extended far behind it, and children and even adults climbed over its inviting triple trunks, leaving shiny patches. On a rustic bench nearby a brass plaque distinguished it as the favorite tree of Elizabeth Barlow Rogers, the founder and at that point the president of the Central Park Conservancy. When I came back to photograph it fourteen years later, the tree—thought to be one of the oldest in the park— had slipped seamlessly back into the woods behind it. Branches of other trees had been allowed to grow out around it, seedlings and root suckers sprouted in the mulched soil beneath it, a fence protected it, and the rustic bench with its brass plaque had been moved to the other side of the clearing. "Sometimes people will love something to death," said Neil Calvanese, vice president for operations in Central Park. "They want to really go up to a tree and everything gets trampled. There was too much time being spent there." Black tupelo is a local native species that can grow very old. The tree author Ned Barnard told me he had cored specimens on Long Island that were three hundred years old and had seen one that was said to be seven hundred. Like sassafras, black tupelo tends to sprout from root suckers. Because this one grows among rocks and lacks a central trunk, it probably sprouted on its own as a "volunteer." Some think it may even predate the park. The best time to visit it is late fall, when the leaves, still greenish-yellow in the picture, turn a shocking red.

Post Oak *Quercus stellata* 20"
Hunter Island, Pelham Bay Park, Bronx
March 7, 2012

Dendrochronologists, who determine the ages of trees from their rings, are the wet blankets of the tree world, constantly pricking assumptions and deflating exaggerations with their incontrovertible woody findings. But sometimes their discoveries have the opposite effect. Take the post oaks in Pelham Bay Park, unassuming trees at the northern edge of their range that have made a place for themselves along the edges of Hunter and Twin Islands despite constant buffeting by the wind and salt spray from the Long Island Sound (settlers used this tough wood for fence posts and forts). In his rambles around the city, the tree author Ned Barnard had noticed these diminutive trees and become curious about them. He obtained permission from the Parks Department for a dendrochronologist from the Tree-Ring Lab at Columbia University, Neil Pederson, to bore holes in a selection of them and extract cores whose rings could be counted under a microscope. On a hot morning in July Dr. Pederson joined two Parks officials in the forests of Hunter and Twin and cored twenty-two post oaks. It turned out to be an all-day job during which mosquitoes continually attacked dendrochronologist and city officials and poison ivy restricted access to trunks. Halfway through, the officials left and Pederson finished alone, though not without company of the other unexpected kinds one sometimes gets in parks. It turned out to be "one of the most memorable days of fieldwork I've ever had." After mounting the twenty-two cores and reviewing them under a microscope, Pederson found that two of the trees dated back to the early 1770s and others to the beginning of the American Revolution. The trees had already been growing here, he realized, when the British passed through on October 18, 1776, during the Battle of Pell's Point. Many other trees, by their height and girth and grand appearance, might appear more ancient, but in fact these little post oaks, ignored for more than two centuries, turned out to be the oldest living documented trees in New York City.

Katsura Trees *Cercidiphyllum japonicum*
Kissena Park Historic Grove, Flushing, Queens
May 21, 2009

This group of Katsura trees formed a solid wall when foresters first disentangled them from the invasive vines that surrounded them in 1981. When I first photographed them in the late 1990s they still formed a wall, like a stockade fence with branches. Still growing in the row in which they had been planted very closely more than a hundred years earlier, when this section of the park was part of the Parsons nurseries (see page 110), they eventually started to outcompete one another for space and their number began to diminish, leaving gaps in the wall. The canopy continued to spread out, however, filling the gaps left by the missing trees. Paleobotanists have identified fossils of Katsura trees that grew in North America and Europe about 7 million years ago. The species failed to survive the last ice age and died out and today is considered native only in Japan and parts of China. Sometime during the 1860s Thomas Hogg, who had been appointed an American consul to Japan by President Lincoln, sent seeds of the plant back to his brother in New York, who ran a family nursery business. The brother gave or sold some of these seeds to the Parsons nurseries here in Flushing, and it was from those seeds that some of the first Katsura in this country were propagated for sale. This group in the historic grove at Kissena Park probably represents a second generation of the tree in this country, grown from seeds from that first planting. As part of its program to preserve the genetic stock of the city's Great Trees, the Parks Department has cloned them and will eventually plant the cloned specimens around the five boroughs. Like that of the broad, spreading American hornbeam in Prospect Park (page 56), the canopy formed by the arching branches of the Katsura trees suggests a kind of chapel, and I have often arrived to find brides and grooms standing together under the trees, straining anxiously toward kneeling photographers. The small, heart-shaped leaves turn a brilliant orange-yellow in the fall. On the ground, the leaves give off a not unpleasing smell of cotton candy.

White Oak *Quercus alba* 64.5" (Removed 2012)
Split Rock Golf Course, Pelham Bay Park, Bronx
April 23, 2009

Over the years many of us had assumed, from its size and species, that the white oak at the ninth hole of the Split Rock Golf Course had been growing here since the American Revolution. Stone walls still standing on the golf course provided cover for American soldiers as they methodically retreated from the British during the Battle of Pell's Point, and it was curious to think that the tree might have been standing here then as well, absorbing the smoke of battle. We may never know. One of the largest of its kind in the city and, until about ten years ago, one of the most picturesque and dramatic, the tree fell during Hurricane Sandy in 2012. Everyone who played at Split Rock knew the tree, as did many other New Yorkers. I featured it in my 2000 *Guide*. When it began to fail, tree lovers noticed and so did the managers of the golf course, who had to make sure that a branch didn't fall and hurt somebody. To protect the golfers, but also to try to save the tree, the Parks Department undertook a huge preservation effort, pruning the dead branches and supporting the rest with cables. If the tree had been alone in the woods, protected by younger trees pushing in around it, it might have lingered many years longer, slowly senescing into oblivion. But out in this exposed spot, with nearly two-thirds of its branches removed, each puff of wind struck the remaining branches with that much more force. Without the other branches its balance was thrown off, and it was only a matter of time before something would happen. In the hurricane, the tree broke at the base and fell toward the woods on the left, outside the frame of the picture. The roots had begun to rot, and the remaining branches had been unable to steady it during the high winds. Parks officials hoped to hire a dendrochronologist to find out the age of the tree but remained unsure just how much information the compromised wood would reveal. Whatever it does reveal should prove interesting. The agency had cloned the tree some years before and, coincidentally, planned to plant some of its offspring around the city in 2013. Perhaps one will be planted here.

Common Horsechestnut *Aesculus hippocastanum* 48"

Tappen Park, Stapleton, Staten Island
July 30, 2009

There is a generation of horsechestnuts around the city, with trunks roughly the size of this one, that were all planted in the middle of the nineteenth century. With their rough, purple-gray bark and showy white flowers in early May, horsechestnut trees, native to southeastern Europe, line the boulevards of many European cities. Frederick Law Olmsted planted them in Central Park and in Prospect Park and, most notably, in a stunning allee around Fort Greene Park in Brooklyn. People tend to avoid planting them now because of a fungus, *Guignardia aesculi*, that attacks the leaves and causes them to turn brown, curl up, and die prematurely. Nevertheless, many specimens continue to prosper throughout the city, dropping their inedible chestnut-like conkers, encased in thorny green rinds, each fall. In England, schoolchildren collect and dry these hard, brown seeds, soak them in vinegar to harden, thread them with shoelaces, and swing them at similar contraptions held by other children in the game known as conkers. According to the Parks Department, the property on which this tree grows was originally part of the farm on which Cornelius Vanderbilt grew up. Called Washington Square when the city purchased it in 1867, it was renamed in 1934 for a local infantryman who had been killed in France during World War I. Among the well-known rappers who grew up in a housing project near the park is Ghostface Killah, whose songs referencing the neighborhood include his raunchy 2009 single "Stapleton Sex." During the twenty minutes I stood photographing the tree, a group of boys played soccer on the oval lawn behind it. Their ghostly forms remained on the film, a blur in the background, long after I had left the park and darkness had fallen—four boys playing soccer near an ancient tree in an old town square on a summer evening.

White Mulberry *Morus alba* 45"
Bridle Path near Tennis House, Central Park, Manhattan
February 26, 2010

In recent years severe storms have ripped through parks throughout New York City, bringing down trees left and right. For some reason, they have hit Central Park with particular consistency, and one of their many victims was this white mulberry, which lost a major limb about ten years ago. "It was actually a much more spectacular tree with a much more well-balanced canopy," Neil Calvanese, Central Park's vice president for operations, remembered. "It's still a beauty, but it's kind of lost something." Unlike most of New York City's urban forest (and that includes trees on streets as well as those in parks), trees in Central Park give an almost uniform impression of being individually cared for. Walk up to any specimen not in the Ramble or in the North Woods and you can see where arborists have pruned limbs, removed suckers, loosened the soil underneath, and spread mulch around to combat soil compaction. Each tree seems to be known and understood, as if the 843 acres of the park were a small garden and the trees had been planted intentionally. Of course, many of them were planted intentionally. But a surprisingly large number were not. Quite a few, such as this mulberry, seeded themselves. The juicy, raspberry-like fruit that mulberries produce is extremely popular with birds, and the birds are efficient at dispersing the seeds rapidly and over great distances. "We haven't done any plantings of mulberries in thirty-one years," Calvanese said. For a long time foresters incorrectly classified this tree as a native red mulberry, but Calvanese considers it much more likely a white mulberry, the nonnative species that was imported from China during the nineteenth century in the hope of supporting an American silk industry (see page 58). The nonnative species has been quietly but efficiently supplanting the native one. The steel-and-cast-iron bridge behind this white mulberry is called the Gothic Bridge and was designed by Calvert Vaux and completed in 1864. The England-born Vaux and his assistant Jacob Wrey Mould designed thirty-six bridges in the park. Each is different from the next, yet all now seem essential to the landscape.

Yoshino Cherry *Prunus x yedoensis* 26.5"
East side of Central Park Reservoir at East 89th Street, Manhattan
April 4, 2010

The pinkish-white radiance of the blossoms on this Japanese hybrid cherry, seen early in the morning before the sun has had a chance to introduce its fatal yellows, seems to define all that is good in the notion of pink. First planted on this continent at the Arnold Arboretum in Boston in 1902 and now to be found around the world, Yoshino cherries are thought to descend from a single deliberate cross-breeding of two native Japanese species some time in the eighteenth century. The twenty-seven specimens forming a double row along the bridle path on the east side of the reservoir in Central Park were part of a gift of two thousand cherry trees to the city from the city of Tokyo in 1912. In fact the gift was a replacement for an earlier shipment—sent to commemorate the three hundredth anniversary of Henry Hudson's exploration of the Hudson River and the one hundredth of Robert Fulton's demonstration of the steamboat—that had been lost at sea in 1910. Each April when the blossoms come out (or each March, as occurred in the warm spring of 2012) photographers converge on the bridle path to capture the bright petals, and the dog walkers, runners, and strollers who normally pass by do so a little more slowly. In Japan, the blossoming of the cherries is the time of *hanami*, the cherry blossom viewing festivals. The Japanese have kept the tradition of *hanami* for centuries, and precise dates for the flowering of the cherries have been kept longer than for those of perhaps any other species in the world. These records have been invaluable to scientists measuring climate change. Behind the tree, across Fifth Avenue, barely visible on the right of the picture, is the Guggenheim Museum, designed by Frank Lloyd Wright and opened in 1959. The number of museums surrounding Central Park and even in it (as is the case with the Metropolitan Museum of Art a few blocks to the south) suggests in yet another way the close connection between trees and the city's cultural identity.

White Oak *Quercus alba* 71" (removed September 2009)
233 Arleigh Road, Douglaston, Queens
July 29, 2009

Very early one morning in August 2009, the heavy limb on the left-hand side of this tree broke off and fell onto the house, crushing part of the roof and a patio. The owners of the house, Ray and Ann Rombone, regularly sat on that patio to do their work, and their grandchildren played there. When it was built in 1961, the house had been set unusually far back from the road to accommodate the tree—so far back that it had no backyard. Because of this, the grandchildren often played in the front yard, under the tree. "Most people care about the tree," Mr. Rombone told me when I stopped by after the limb fell. "But I also have to think about my family." The Rombones hired an arborist to examine the tree, and the arborist determined that the tree was rotten. Mr. Rombone and his wife decided to have it cut down. Five men spent three days removing the tree in stages. So rotten was it at the core that the arborist was unable to count the rings and determine its age. While it was coming down, neighbors gathered and reminisced about the tree. A generally accepted legend had been that the tree was six hundred years old, but nobody had ever been able to prove this. The city's Landmarks Preservation Commission had cited that number in its report designating Douglas Manor a historic district in 1997, but nobody knew where the commission members had gotten their information. Dr. Leo Kellerman, a retired physician who had lived in Douglaston for fifty-five years and been head of the Douglas Manor Tree Association, said that the tree had been considered one of the oldest living things on Long Island. In his memory it was first known as the Hoffman Tree, after a family that had lived near it and taken care of it. Children had found arrowheads and pottery around its base and, after digging around more carefully, archaeologists had determined that Native Americans had used it for ceremonial purposes. A developer had wanted to remove the tree, Dr. Kellerman said, but luckily "an elderly woman" had outbid the developer and designed the current house so that it would give plenty of space to the tree. This was what Dr. Kellerman remembered.

Trees of New York City

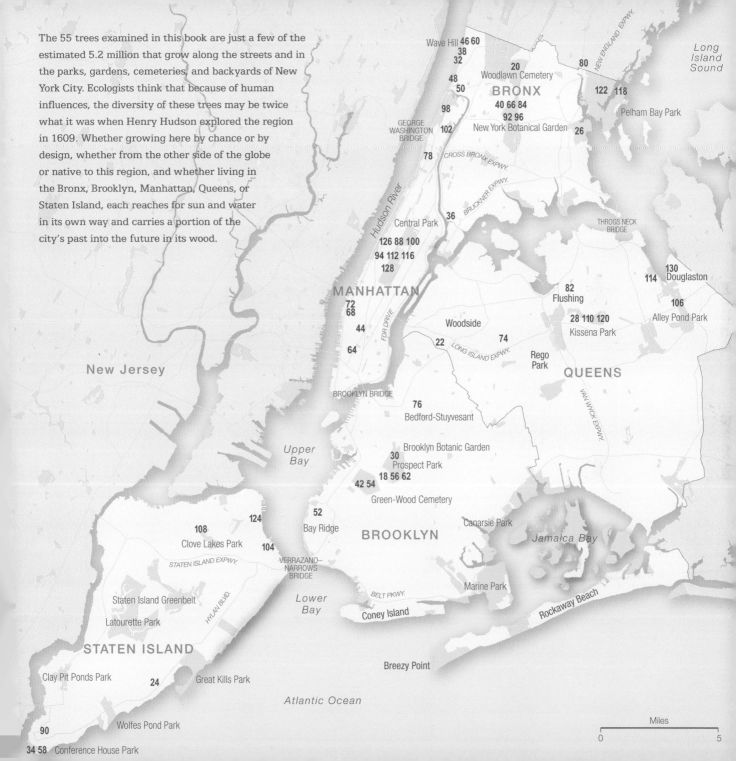

The 55 trees examined in this book are just a few of the estimated 5.2 million that grow along the streets and in the parks, gardens, cemeteries, and backyards of New York City. Ecologists think that because of human influences, the diversity of these trees may be twice what it was when Henry Hudson explored the region in 1609. Whether growing here by chance or by design, whether from the other side of the globe or native to this region, and whether living in the Bronx, Brooklyn, Manhattan, Queens, or Staten Island, each reaches for sun and water in its own way and carries a portion of the city's past into the future in its wood.

Wave Hill 46 60
38
32
20
Woodlawn Cemetery
48
50
BRONX
98
40 66 84
92 96
102
New York Botanical Garden
26
GEORGE
WASHINGTON
BRIDGE
Pelham Bay Park
78
CROSS BRONX EXPWY.
BRUCKNER EXPWY.
Long Island Sound
80
NEW ENGLAND EXPWY.
122 118
THROGS NECK BRIDGE
36
Central Park
130
Douglaston
126 88 100
114
94 112 116
128
82
Flushing
MANHATTAN
72
68
Woodside
28 110 120
106
Alley Pond Park
44
74
Kissena Park
64
22
LONG ISLAND EXPWY.
Rego Park
New Jersey
QUEENS
FDR DRIVE
Hudson River
VAN WYCK EXPWY.
BROOKLYN BRIDGE
76
Bedford-Stuyvesant
Upper Bay
Brooklyn Botanic Garden
30
Prospect Park
18 56 62
42 54
Green-Wood Cemetery
Canarsie Park
52
Bay Ridge
BROOKLYN
Jamaica Bay
108
124
Clove Lakes Park
104
VERRAZANO-
NARROWS
BRIDGE
STATEN ISLAND EXPWY.
Marine Park
Staten Island Greenbelt
HYLAN BLVD.
Lower Bay
BELT PKWY.
Rockaway Beach
Latourette Park
STATEN ISLAND
24
Clay Pit Ponds Park
Great Kills Park
Coney Island
90
Wolfes Pond Park
Breezy Point
Atlantic Ocean
Miles
0   5
34 58 Conference House Park

Acknowledgments

This book could never have been made without the encouragement of many people who contributed in countless ways. For the initial opportunity to photograph trees as part of my job at the Parks Department, and for starting me on the path that led here, I am especially grateful to Henry J. Stern, Deborah Landau, Therese Braddick, Fiona Watt, the late Arthur Ross, and Gail Lloyd.

For sitting with me in subsequent years looking through photographs, riding around looking at trees, giving permission to photograph trees, responding to e-mails, sending articles, or giving time and thought in other ways to helping me visit and understand the trees of New York, I wish to thank Vincent Begley, Thomas Bird, Mark DeFillo, Sarah Kerlin Gund, Ralph Isham, Kristin Jones, Leo Kellerman, Katie Michel, Marian and Wolfgang Radermacher, Ray Rombone, Janet Ross, and Robert Supina; Ned Barnard and Ken Chaya of Central Park Nature; Art Presson and Jeff Richman of Green-Wood Cemetery; John Toale and Susan Olsen of Woodlawn Cemetery; Sara Signorelli of the Alice Austen House; Todd Forrest, Karl Lauby, Jessica Arcate Schuler, and Deanna Curtis of the New York Botanical Garden; Mark Fisher and Christopher Roddick of the Brooklyn Botanic Garden; Charles Day and all my friends at Wave Hill; Deborah Landau and Tom Reidy of the Madison Square Park Conservancy; Doug Blonsky, Neil Calvanese, Sara Cedar Miller, and Betsy Barlow Rogers of the Central Park Conservancy; Danya Sherman and Patrick Cullina of the Friends of the High Line; Richard Hourahan of the Queens Historical Society; Eric W. Sanderson of the Wildlife Conservation Society, Bronx Zoo; Edward Cook and Neil Pederson of the Tree-Ring Laboratory at Columbia University's Lamont-Doherty Earth Observatory; Jinshuang Ma of the Shanghai Chenshan Plant Science Research Center, Chinese Academy of Sciences; William C. Janeway, Tad Norton, and Jeffrey Wiegert of the New York State Department of Environmental Conservation; and Adrian Benepe, Jennifer Greenfeld, Betsy Gotbaum, Bram Gunther, Jamie Hewitt, Liam Kavanagh, Jonathan Kuhn, Jennifer Lantzas, James Lemyre, Morgan Monaco, Steven Rizick, Julius Spiegel, William Steyer, Fiona Watt, Matthew Wells, Veronica White, and Bonnie Williams of New York City Parks and Recreation.

For their enthusiastic support of the project from the start I am grateful to Joan K. Davidson, Michael J. Gladstone, and Ann Birckmayer of Furthermore, and, for their additional help as fiscal agents, Simon Chu, Alison Tocci, and David Rivel of the City Parks Foundation. For reading the manuscript, catching errors, and making numerous helpful suggestions I am indebted to Deanna Curtis of the New York Botanical Garden and Matthew Wells of New York City Parks and Recreation. Any mistakes not discovered by these thoughtful readers are mine alone.

This is my third book published by The Quantuck Lane Press and I feel lucky to remain connected with such a distinguished, kind, and imaginative publisher as James Mairs. Associate publisher Austin O'Driscoll, copy editor Donald Kennison, and master designer Laura Lindgren made the book as clean and beautiful as it is, while Myra Klockenbrink continued to add new dimensions to my work with her cartography. It was Timothy Seldes, my agent, who first brought me to Quantuck Lane, and Christina Shideler who made sure I stayed there.

For their help from the very beginning with choices of text and photographs and for their understanding of what I have been trying to do, I wish to acknowledge George Prochnik, Harry Wilks, and Katherine Swett. For their help in a larger sense during these years I could not have done without my friends and family. To Katherine, to our sons, Nicholas and William, and in memory of our dear daughter Rachel I dedicate this book.

Specific credits, sources, and comments follow. If not directly noted, botanical information can be assumed to come from one or more of four main sources: Barnard (2002), Burns and Honkala (1990), Dirr (2009), and Sternberg (2004). Likewise, unless otherwise noted, information on the history of parks derives from two authorities: the Parks and Recreation park pages at www .nycgovparks.org, first organized by Commissioner Henry J. Stern and Jonathan Kuhn as the Historical Signs Project; and the Parks and Recreation Map Files at the Olmsted Center in Flushing Meadows–Corona Park, under the jurisdiction of Steven Rizick.

Notes

Pages 9–15. Harrison's and Schama's monumental works directly address the idea of trees as storehouses of the past, but their broad focus is on Western cultural and literary history rather than on specific urban forests such as New York City's. Barnard, Curtis, Forrest, Pederson, Sanderson, and Wells all discussed and reviewed various parts of the introduction with me. Papers by Nowak and colleagues at the USDA on New York City's urban forest and evaluating urban forests in general were helpful. Sanderson's view of historical Mannahatta (and by extension New York City as a whole) as a series of "ecological neighborhoods" supports the idea of the contemporary urban forest as a conglomeration of trees from disparate places that serve unique functions in the particular places where they grow. The latest tree count is from Peper et al. (2007). The story of the Caucasian wingnuts in Iran is from Akhani and Salimian (2003). The Harrison reference is from Harrison (1992). Sadly, a misunderstanding by a supervisor at a Parks Department storage facility on Randall's Island in 2012 led to the destruction of almost all remaining copies of my 2000 book.

18. Camperdown elm. Olson's original research (2011) on A. A. Burgess, on the background of Moore's involvement with the elm, and on the various critical responses to Moore's poem was instrumental here. The 1935 diameter and pipe-rail information are from Map #B-T-73-113, dated November 14, 1935, in the Parks and Recreation Map Files.

20. Weeping beech. Susan Olsen of Woodlawn Cemetery provided a scan of the 1914 photograph. Details on and the quotation about the Gould burials are from the *New York Times* (1889, 1892) and information on Gould himself from the *Brooklyn Daily Eagle* (1892). Background on the weeping beech and the Parsons family, including the quotation about the beech, are from the City of New York/Parks and Recreation park pages.

22. Common pear. Mr. and Mrs. Radermacher very kindly allowed me access to the tree, their garden, and their lives (2010). The story of the Stuyvesant pear is recounted most thoroughly in Rosenstock (2005).

24. Olmsted-Beil osage orange. DeFillo (2010). *Daily Plant* (2006). City Planning Commission resolution (2004).

26. White oak. On the dominance of chestnuts before European arrival, Sanderson (2009). On making flour from acorns, Sanderson and most thoroughly Logan (2005). On the current condition of the tree, Wells (2009, 2012). On Pelham Bay Park history, Parks and Recreation park pages.

28. Persian parrotia. The New York Botanical Garden also has three impressive specimens planted in 1906. The quotation is from Nicholson (1989). Wells provided the 1936 map and Rizick the 1935 one (City of New York/Parks and Recreation Map Files, map #Q-T-24-104).

30. Caucasian wingnut. The paper by Akhani and Salimian (2003) studies a distinct natural stand of *Pterocarya fraxinifolia* in a village in the central Zagros Mountains. "According to the local community," the authors write, "the Pterocarya fraxinifolia trees grow here with living memory and the belief that cutting is inauspicious has preserved them to the present." Information on Michaux from the Williams sketch (2002). Analysis of current condition of tree from personal observation and Roddick (2011, 2012, 2012).

32. Cucumber magnolia. Information on Greyston, the Dodge family, and Gilbert Kerlin from the *New York Times* (1987, 2004), Gund (2011, 2012), and Michel (2012).

34. Conference House sycamore. The story and background on the conference are from McCullough (2002), 155. On the National Register of Big Trees, the largest sycamore in the United States, in Ashland, Ohio, has a diameter of 134 inches based on a circumference of 422 inches. When I measured it in 2009, the Pynchot sycamore in Simsbury, Connecticut, had a diameter of 106 inches.

36. Bruckner Boulevard elm. The USDA has published numerous papers on the valuation of trees in cities—some helpful ones being Dwyer et al. (1992) and Nowak et al. (2002). Both Steyer and Watt alluded specifically to New York City's valuation methods in their correspondence with me about the Eleventh Avenue Callery pear (see note for pages 68–70).

38. European beech. *New York Times*, August 21 and November 11, 1918, and November 16, 1987.

40. Royal paulownia. "Weeds Gone Wild" (2010), Forrest (2010), Curtis (2012).

42. Camperdown elm. Presson (2011, 2012), Richman (2011, 2012). Map of the Green-Wood Cemetery (2009).

44. Madison Square elm. Steyer, Manhattan's director of forestry and horticulture, has been working at Parks since 1981 and knew the elm well. "To me it was such an unbelievable specimen," he said. Heartbroken at its loss, he "left a monument out of it for a while so we could say farewell" (Steyer, 2012). Historical information on tree and park from Steyer (2012) and Berman (2001); information on condition of tree from Watt et al. (2010) and Steyer (2012). On fashions in tree planting: Barnard, Calvanese, Campanella, Day, Pederson, Sanderson, and Watt et al. all supported this idea in interviews or articles. Historical diameter from City of New York/Parks and Recreation Map Files, M-T-43-101, 1934.

46. Lacebark pine. The 1996 diameter is from Kenney (1996). The English-language Web sites of several Beijing tour companies repeat the story of the irrigation tunnel, but the article by Moller (2004) is the most authoritative. Information on this specimen is from Day (2010) and on that in the New York Botanical Garden from Forrest (2012). Pederson (2012) provided the Hudson Valley rainfall data.

48. Spuyten Duyvil tuliptree. Bird (2009).

50. Corlear Avenue sycamore. During the interview in his apartment in Riverdale, Mr. Snowden showed me photographs of Mayor Koch and a young Henry Stern at the June 18, 1983, event. The quotation from Mr. Lese is from the *New York Times* (2000). Prices are from the Web site "Sycamore Court Condos," and other background from Judd (2008) and the O'Flynn brothers (2011).

52. Bay Ridge elm. The quotations are from the article by "Stranger" in the *Brooklyn Daily Eagle* (1873). Additional material is from Squitieri et al. (2008), which I believe to have been compiled for a class assignment for the Macauley Honors Program at Brooklyn College, and Scarpa and Stelter (2009), whose evocative photograph from the Bay Ridge Historical Society of a streetcar on Third Avenue at 75th Street (one block from our elm) gives a good sense of how thickly those trees were planted, and how muddy the streets could become.

54. Sassafras. Presson, the superintendent of grounds at Green-Wood, showed me these specimens almost as an afterthought. Information on the Central Park sassafras is from Barnard, Chaya, and personal observation. Richman, the Green-Wood historian, explained the headstones.

56. American hornbeam. The 1967 letter by Moore to M. M. Graff is quoted by Olson (2011). The 1996 diameter is from Kenney (1996). For what it's worth, the hornbeam also appears on the same 1935 map as the Camperdown elm (B-T-73-113—see note for page 18) as "6 ironwood trunks."

58. White mulberry. The quotations are from Dirr (2009), Kieran (1959), and, most thoroughly, McCullough (2002), 156–57.

60. Copper beech. Day (2012), Wells (2012), Curtis (2012).

62. Silver linden. The quotation is from Nabokov (1971). The historical diameter is from Map #B-T 73-109-1935 in the City of New York/Parks and Recreation Map Files.

64. Washington Square elm. Historical information on the park is from the "Washington Square" page on the City of New York/Parks and Recreation Web site, "Washington Square New York City" (2011), and Geismer (2005), whose 95-page report, prepared for a park reconstruction, is the most thorough investigation of the park's physical history I have found. Information on the Ludlow property is from pages 8–12, 15, 24, 25, and 43 of that report. The historical diameter is from Map #M-T-98-100 in the City of New York/Parks and Recreation Map Files. For the record, in the spring of 2012 I counted ninety rings in a 13-inch-diameter limb pruned from the very top of this enormous tree.

66. Snake branch spruce. Forrest (2010), "Montgomery's History" (2010).

68–70. Callery pears. Count of Manhattan Callery pear trees in City of New York/Parks and Recreation, 2005–2006 Street Tree Census. There is no more authoritative description of Callery pears than Barnard (2002), but I have also drawn on Dirr (2009). I learned the background of the removal in Watt (2008) and also in the e-mail she attached from Steyer (2008).

72. Ailanthus. Species sample by Nowak et al. (2007). Pan and Bassuk (1986) have concluded that the ability of ailanthus to outcompete other species in urban areas throughout the United States is due to its simple root system of "a few flexible lateral roots and a large tap root." Cullina (2011) and Sherman (2011) of the Friends of the High Line confirmed the removal of this ailanthus and explained the replacement of ailanthus with sumac.

74. Honeylocust. In 2012 I encountered some formidable thorns on a honey locust with a 62-inch diameter growing beside the front steps of Cedar Grove, Thomas Cole's house in Catskill, New York. The thorns were like porcupine quills, only thankfully not barbed, or grizzly bear claws. They were deadly sharp. According to our guide, the Cedar Grove tree was one of an original twelve planted in 1815—back, she said, when planting honey locusts on your lawn was considered a sign of affluence.

76. Southern magnolia. Some other trees in the city have achieved landmark status but not as individual specimens. The white oak in Douglaston, Queens, was included in the Douglas Manor Historic District in 1997 (see page 130), and the famous tuliptree allee at the New York Botanical Garden (not, unfortunately, in this book) was named a landmark along with the library building and fountain in 2009. The story of Carthan, the tree, and the landmarking of the tree are from Landmarks Preservation Commission (1970) and the City of New York/Parks and Recreation park pages for "Magnolia Tree Earth Center" and "Hattie Carthan Garden."

78. St. Nicholas Avenue elm. Speculation about this tree will never end. Information on the Morrises and their house and land comes from the City of New York/Parks and Recreation park pages, and on possible connections between the Morrises and the tree from Hellman (1990), Watt et al. (2010), and Barnard (2011). Wartime occupation of the Morris house and possible effects on trees are from McCullough (2005), 216–31, and Sanderson (2009).

80. Westchester County royal paulownia. The Fairway Web site (2012) and the *New York Times* (2011) say it all.

82. Cedar of Lebanon. Richard Hourahan, collections manager at the Queens Historical Society, gave planting information. Google produces many pictures of earlier Flushing cedars but most haunting (because we know so little else about it) is in Murch (1917). Information on cedars from Aiello (2007), Dirr (2009), and Habeeb.com.

84–86. Dawn redwoods. The section on the dawn redwood draws on Forrest (2010) and, heavily, on original research by Jinshuang Ma (2003, 2003), vice director of the Shanghai Chenshan Plant Science Research Center, Chinese Academy of Sciences, at the Shanghai Chenshan Botanical Garden. Dr. Ma, who worked for many years at the Brooklyn Botanic Garden and who oversees the Web site metasequoia.org, painstakingly recovered the original records of the discovery of the living trees.

88. East Meadow American elm. Quotations and references are from Dame and Brooks (1890), Calvanese (2012), and Barnard (2011).

90. Staten Island cottonwood. The quotation is from Dirr (2009). It's funny how tree experts all seem to dislike at least one species. Information about the houses from Supina (2010) and Digerolamo (2011). In terms of the ages of cottonwoods, a "chain of documentation" and memories of a core sample taken in 1953 date a standing eastern cottonwood at Balmville in Orange County, New York, to 1699. In far worse condition than the Tottenville tree, supported by wires and under constant surveillance by the New York State Department of Environmental Conservation, this ancient cottonwood continues to stand at a busy intersection. See Luley (1994) and Sebesta (1999). I'm grateful to my cousin W. C. Janeway of the DEC for alerting me to this extraordinary tree.

92. Tanyosho pine. The conifer arboretum is now named for Arthur and Janet Ross, whose interest in the city's trees has extended not only to pines (see page

112) but also to elms: a Dutch elm disease–resistant Chinese elm cultivar named *Ulmus parvifolia 'A. Ross Central Park'* was named for Mr. Ross, who funded work on it, and has been planted around the world. Information on the tanyoshos is from Forrest (2010) and on Japanese gardens from Wright and Katsuhiko (1990).

94. Humboldt elm. Calvanese (2012), Kuhn (2012). Count of elms in Central Park from Chaya and Barnard (2011).

96. European hornbeam. Dirr (2009), Day (2012), Forrest (2010, 2012).

98. Isham Park ginkgo. On ginkgoes, Jonnes (2011), Dirr (2009). On Manhattan ginkgoes, City of New York/ Parks and Recreation Street Tree Census (2006). On Isham Park and its ginkgo, City of New York/Parks and Recreation, "Isham Park," Isham (2012), and Begley (2012).

100. Runners' Gate English elm. Barnard (2011), Calvanese (2012), Steyer (2012).

102. Harlem River Drive elm. On elms, Burns and Honkala (1990). On Moses, *New York Times* (1981). On Highbridge, City of New York/Parks and Recreation park pages and nycroads.com (2011, 2012). Planting record from City of New York/Parks and Recreation Map Files, Map #M-T-37-106-1934.

104. Alice Austen sycamore. Although Sara Signorelli of the Alice Austen House tried, she was unable to locate a photograph by Austen that included the tree. I am still hopeful to find one some day in the collection of Austen's work at the Staten Island Historical Society. Background information on Austen is from aliceausten. org and the City of New York/Parks and Recreation park pages.

106. Alley Pond Park tuliptree. The absence of this tree from my 2000 book led to the article by Crewdson

and Mittelbach (2000) comparing this and the Clove Lakes tree. Over the years I've spoken about the tree with many, especially Ned Barnard, Jennifer Greenfeld, and Neil Pederson. Some background is from the *New York Times* (2009). Pederson gave me a printout of his rainfall survey during our interview (2012). Historical diameter from City of New York/ Parks and Recreation Map Files, Map #Q-T-1-136-R 1943.

108. Clove Lakes Park tuliptree. The story of the privet hedge and the railway tunnel is from the City of New York/Parks and Recreation Map Files, Map #R-T-5-11, June 1934. As described in *The Daily Plant* (2008), the neighboring tuliptree contained a large beehive at 60 feet when it was taken down. Ed Cook's comment is from his e-mail (2012). No discussion of tuliptrees in New York City can fail to include the extraordinary double allee in front of the library at the New York Botanical Garden, declared, along with the library and its fountain, a New York City landmark in 2009.

110. Kissena Park beeches. Hellman (1990), Wells (2010), Abramson (2010), and the City of New York/ Parks and Recreation park pages.

112. Arthur Ross Pinetum. Peterson (2004), Barnard (2011), Miller (2012), Calvanese (2012), Ross (2012).

114. Crocheron Park osage oranges. Botanical history is from Barlow (2001). T shape recorded by Kenney (1996).

116. Black tupelo. I first visited the tree with my daughter and her friend in 1996, when they were seven. They parked their scooters at the base and chased each other around the tree trunks and climbed the trunks. The shininess of the bark was thus partially the result of their antics, which filled a full contact sheet. Particulars on this specimen from Barnard (2011) and Calvanese (2012).

118. Pelham Bay Park post oak. Older trees have been documented but cannot be included in the current count. Paul R. Sheppard and Jessica Arcate Schuler cored some eastern hemlocks, since lost to the woolly adelgid, in the Forest at the New York Botanical Garden in 1985 and dated them to the 1750s (Sheppard and Cook, 1985). A red oak still growing in that forest is also said to have been cored around that time and dated to 1735, but the records have been lost (Forrest, 2012). The post oak coring story was related to me in person, by e-mail, and in published articles by all involved: Barnard (2011), Watt et al. (2010), Gunther (2004), and Pederson (2012, 2012).

120. Katsura trees. Paleobotany is from Brown (1939). History on trees and park from Lewis (1976), Barnard (2002), and Parks and Recreation park page for "Kissena Grove."

122. Split Rock white oak. I am indebted to Wells for ideas (Wells, 2009) about how branches absorb wind and mitigate tension, having discussed this tree over many years with Wells, Watt, Greenfeld, Barnard, and Steyer.

124. Tappen Park horsechestnut. Nobody under thirty should listen to the song. Information on the park is from the City of New York/Parks and Recreation park page.

126. Tennis House white mulberry. Calvanese (2012), Barnard (2011), Dirr (2009). "A good fifty percent of the mulberries in Central Park are self-planted," said Ned Barnard.

128. Yoshino cherry. History of these specimens is primarily from the Parks and Recreation park page for Sakura Park, where trees from the 1912 shipment also grow. On cherry blossoms and climate change, Primack and Higuchi (2007).

130. Douglaston white oak. This tree has been discussed and written about by many. One of my most memorable visits was in 2002 with Fiona Watt and Thomas Packenham, who was in New York to promote *Remarkable Trees of the World*. Mr. Packenham gazed long and hard at the oak but said little. I had a feeling that even if it did turn out to be six hundred years old it still somehow wouldn't quite measure up to his standards. The quotation is from Rombone (2009), and much in the section is from my memorable interview with Dr. Kellerman that same day.

Bibliography and Sources

Abramson, P. E-mail to the author. February 17, 2010.

Aiello, A. S., and Dosmann, M. S. 2007. "The Quest for the Hardy Cedar-of-Lebanon." *Arnoldia* 65/1, pp. 26–35.

Akhani, H., and Salimian, M. 2003. "An extant disjunct stand of Pterocarya fraxinifolia (Juglandaceae) in the central Zagros Mountains, W. Iran." *Willdenowia*, pp. 33: 113–20.

Aliceausten.org. "Alice Austen." http://aliceausten.org/alice-austen/.

Anderson, E. 1933. *Pterocarya rehderiana*. Arnold Arboretum, Harvard University. *Bulletin of Popular Information*, series 4, vol. 1, no. 11, pp. 57–60.

Barlow, Connie. 2001. "Anachronistic Fruits and the Ghosts Who Haunt Them." *Arnoldia* 61/2, pp. 14–21.

Barnard, Edward Sibley. 2002. *New York City Trees: A Field Guide for the Metropolitan Area.* New York: Columbia University Press.

——. Telephone interview. March 29, 2011.

——. E-mail to the author. October 26, 2011.

Begley, Vincent. Unpublished research on the Isham family. Prepared for Ralph Isham. Received July 10, 2012.

——. E-mail to Ralph Isham. July 11, 2011.

Berman, M. 2001. *Madison Square: The Park and Its Celebrated Landmarks.* Salt Lake City: Gibbs Smith.

Bird, Thomas. Personal interview. June 1, 2009.

Brown, R. W. 1939. "Fossil Leaves, Fruits, and Seeds of Cercidiphyllum." *Journal of Paleontology*, vol. 13, no. 5, pp. 485–99.

Burns, R. M., and Honkala, Barbara H. tech. coords. 1990. *Silvics of North America: 1. Conifers; 2. Hardwoods.* Agriculture Handbook 654. U.S. Department of Agriculture, Forest Service, Washington, DC, vol. 2, at http://www.na.fs.fed.us/spfo/pubs/silvics_manual/table_of_contents.htm.

Calvanese, Neil. Personal interview. January 26, 2012.

Campanella, T. J. "The Roman Roots of Gotham's London Plane," *Wall Street Journal*, July 20, 2011.

Chaya, K. E-mail to the author. November 7, 2011.

———, and Barnard, E. S. 2011. *Central Park Entire: The Definitive Illustrated Folding Map*. New York: Central Park Nature.

City of New York/Parks and Recreation, Map File. The Olmsted Center, Flushing Meadows–Corona Park, Queens. Visited June 8, 2011.

———, park pages, http://www.nycgovparks.org/. "Harlem River Drive," accessed October 26, 2011. "Isham Park," accessed February 27, 2010. "Magnolia Tree Earth Center," B400/ highlights/11891, accessed November 22, 2011. "Morris-Jumel Mansion" and "Morris-Jumel Mansion, Roger Morris Park," accessed February 8, 2010. "Raoul Wallenberg Forest," X259/ highlights/9769, accessed May 19, 2012.

———, 2005–2006 Street Tree Census, http://www.nycgovparks.org/trees/tree-census/2005-2006. Accessed May 20, 2012.

City Planning Commission. 2004. Resolution C 010656 MMR. July 14, 2004/Calendar No. 30.

Cook, Edward. E-mail to the author. February 28, 2012.

Crewdson, M.,and Mittelbach, M. 2000. "A Rendezvous with 2 Giants," *New York Times*, September 11, 2000.

Cullina, Patrick. E-mail to the author. April 18, 2011.

Curtis, Deanna. Personal interview. June 15, 2012.

The Daily Plant. "Parks Acquires Former Home of Central Park Designer," September 28, 2006. "The Great Tuliptree and the Honeybees," February 21, 2008. Newsletter of the City of New York/Parks and Recreation, at http://www.nycgovparks.org/news/daily-plant?id=19949.

Dame, L. L., and Brooks, Henry. 1890. "The American Elm." Reprinted from *Typical Elms and Other Trees of Massachusetts* (Boston: Little Brown), in *Arnoldia* 42/2, Spring 1982.

Day, Charles. Personal interviews. January 8, 2010, and March 6, 2012.

———. E-mails to the author. March 7, 2012, and June 29, 2012.

Day, Leslie. 2011. *Field Guide to the Street Trees of New York City.* Baltimore: Johns Hopkins.

DeFillo, Mark. Personal interview. February 5, 2010.

Digerolamo, Dennis. Personal interview. June 2, 2011.

Dirr, Michael A. 2009. *Manual of Woody Landscape Plants: Their Identification, Ornamental Characteristics, Culture, Propagation and Uses*, sixth edition. Champaign, Illinois: Stipes Publishing.

Dwyer, John F., E. G. McPherson, H. W. Schroeder, R. A. Rountree. 1992. "Assessing the Benefits and Costs of the Urban Forest." *Journal of Arboriculture* 18(5).

———, H. W. Schroeder, P. H. Gobster. 1990. "The Significance of Urban Trees and Forests: Toward a Deeper Understanding of Values." Paper for the Sustainable Cities Symposium: Preserving and Restoring Urban Biodiversity, Chicago Academy of Sciences, October 4–6, 1990.

FairwayMarket.com. "Pelham Manor, New York— Fairway Market," at http://www.fairwaymarket.com/store-pelham-manor/. Accessed April 3, 2012.

Fisher, Mark. Personal interview. October 29, 2009.

Forrest, Todd. Personal interview. January 5, 2010.

———. E-mails to the author. February 11 and 17, 2010; April 5 and July 5, 2012.

Geismer, Joan H. 2005. "Washington Square Park: Phase 1A Archaeological Assessment." Prepared through Thomas Baisley and Associates for the New York City Department of Parks and Recreation.

Greenfield, Jennifer. Personal interviews. May 11, 2011, and May 16, 2012.

Gund, Sarah Kerlin. E-mails to the author. December 12 and 13, 2011; January 24, 2012.

Gunther, Bram. 2004. "Post Oaks in Pelham Bay Park." Mr. Beller's Neighborhood: New York Stories. http://mrbellersneighborhood.com/2004/09/post-oaks-in-pelham-bay-park. September 27, 2004.

——. Personal interview. May 16, 2012.

Habeeb.com. 2006. "Cedars of Lebanon-History," at www.habeeb.com/cedar.of.lebanon/cedar.of.lebanon. info.html. Accessed October 28, 2011.

Harrison, Robert Pogue. 1993. *Forests: The Shadow of Civilization*. Chicago: University of Chicago Press.

Hellman, Gordon. 1990. *Great Tree Walk Guide*. New York: City of New York/Parks and Recreation.

Hourahan, Richard. Telephone interview. November 3, 2011.

Isham, Ralph. E-mails to the author. July 10 and 11, 2012.

"Jay Gould Died Today," *Brooklyn Daily Eagle*, December 2, 1892.

Jonnes, Jill. 2011. "The Living Dinosaur: Peter Del Tredici's Search for the Wild Ginkgo." *Harvard Magazine*, November–December 2011, pp. 31–91.

Judd, N. Clark. "Condo Builder Vows to Save Ancient Tree." *Riverdale Press*, June 19, 2008.

Kellerman, Leo. Personal interview. September 2, 2009.

Kenney, Kevin C. 1996. "Great Trees of New York City." Elmsford, NY: F.A. Bartlett Tree Expert Co. Report for the City of New York/Parks & Recreation.

Kieran, John. 1959. *A Natural History of New York City*. Boston: Houghton Mifflin Co.

Kuhn, Jonathan. E-mail to the author. February 3, 2012.

Landmarks Preservation Commission. 1970. Landmark Designation. July 12, 1970, Number 1. LP-0641. "Magnolia Grandiflora, 679 Lafayette Avenue, Borough of Brooklyn, c. 1885."

Lewis, C. E. "Our American Heritage—Trees." *Journal of Arboriculture*, vol. 2, no. 10, October 1976.

Logan, William Bryant. 2005. *Oak: The Frame of Civilization*. New York: W. W. Norton.

Luley, Christopher J. *The Balmville Tree Report*. Rochester, NY: ACRT. August 31, 1994.

Ma, Jinshuang. "The Chronology of the 'Living Fossil' Metasequoia Glyptostroboides (Taxodiaceae): A Review (1943–2003)." Harvard Papers in Botany, vol. 8, no 1, 2003, pp. 9–18.

——, and Guofan Shao. "Rediscovery of the 'First Collection' of the 'Living Fossil,' Metasequoia glyptostroboides." *Taxon* 52, August 2003, pp. 585–88.

Map of the Green-Wood Cemetery. 2009. Brooklyn: Green-Wood Historic Fund.

McCullough, David. 2002. *John Adams*. New York: Simon and Schuster.

——. 2005. *1776*. New York: Simon and Schuster.

Michel, Katie. E-mail to the author. January 23, 2012.

Miller, Sara Cedar. Telephone interview. April 26, 2012.

Moller, Daragh. 2004. "Ancient Lacebark General Gives Up Secrets of the Past." In Beijing This Month, http://www.btmbeijing.com/contents/en/btm/2004-08/KYB/water.

"Montgomery's History." 2010. From the Web site of the Montgomery Botanical Center, Coral Gables, Florida. http://www.montgomerybotanical.org/pages/hist.

Moore, Marianne. "The Camperdown Elm." *The New Yorker*. September 23, 1967, p. 48.

Murch, Charles H. 1917. "The Trees of Flushing." *Country Life*, November, 1917, pp. 88–90.

Nabokov, Vladimir. 1971. *Glory*. Trans. by Dmitri Nabokov and the author. New York: McGraw-Hill.

New York Times. "The Yellow Fever," September 1, 1856. "Mrs. Gould's Funeral," January 17, 1889. "Jay Gould's Body at Rest," December 7, 1892. "Douglas Will Filed; Leaves $20,000,000," August 21, 1918. "Bronx Gets Record Tax," November 11, 1918. "Robert Moses, Master Builder, Is Dead at 92," Paul Goldberger, July 30, 1981. "A Renwick Design; Gothic Revival in Riverdale," Lisa W. Foderaro, June 28, 1987. "Bronx Residents Fighting Plans of a Developer," David W. Dunlap, November 16, 1987. "In Kingsbridge, a Sycamore

Faces an Unwelcome Neighbor," Rose McElroy, October 1, 2000. "A Rendezvous with 2 Giants," Michael Crewdson and Margaret Mittelbach, November 10, 2000. "Gilbert Kerlin, Riverdale Conservator, Dies," Stuart Lavietes, April 12, 2004. "The City's Oldest Tree? Who Knows? But Here's a Guess," A. G. Sulzberger, October 7, 2009. "A Scenic Village that Knew What it Wanted, and Got it," Elisa Brenner. May 12, 2010.

Nicholson, Robert G. 1989. "Parrotia Persica: An Ancient Tree for Modern Landscapes." *Arnoldia* 49/4, pp. 34–39.

Nowak, David J. 1993. "Compensatory Value of an Urban Forest: An Application of the Tree-Value Formula." *Journal of Arboriculture* 19(3), pp. 173–77.

——, Crane, D. E., Dwyer, John F. 2002. "Compensatory Value of Urban Trees in the United States." *Journal of Arboriculture* 28(4), July 2002, 194–99.

——, Hoehn, R. E., Crane, D. E., Stevens, J. C., Walton, J. T. 2007. "Assessing Urban Forest Effects and Values: New York City's Urban Forest." Research Bulletin NRS-9. USDA Forest Service, Newtown Square, Pennsylvania.

Nycroads.com. "Harlem River Drive," accessed October 26, 2011; "High Bridge (Aqueduct Bridge)," accessed May 14, 2012. http://www.nycroads.com.

O'Flynn, Patrick and Philip. Personal interviews. May 6 and September 30, 2011.

Olson, Kirby. 2011. "Marianne Moore's 'The Camperdown Elm' and the Revival of Brooklyn's Prospect Park." *Journal of Ecocriticism* 3(20), July 2011, pp. 16–27.

"Outside Views of Brooklyn: Some of Its Suburban Places as Seen by a Stranger," *Brooklyn Daily Eagle*, August 14, 1873, p. 3.

Pan, Elizabeth, and Bassuk, Nina. 1986. *Journal of Environmental Horticulture* 4, pp. 1–4.

Packenham, Thomas. 1996. *Meetings with Remarkable Trees*. New York: Random House.

——. 2002. *Remarkable Trees of the World*. New York: W. W. Norton.

Pederson, Neil. 2010. "External Characteristics of Old Trees in the Eastern Deciduous Forest." *Natural Areas Journal* 30 (4), pp. 396–406.

——. Personal interviews. March 6, 2012, and June 29, 2012.

——. E-mails to the author. April 3, 2012, February 8, 2012 (copy of e-mail originally sent July 29, 2003), April 27, 2012, July 5, 2012, July 6, 2012.

Peper, P. J., E. G. McPherson, J. R. Simpson, S. L. Gardner, K. E. Vargas, Q. Xiao. 2007. "City of New York, New York Municipal Forest Resource Analysis." Center for Urban Forest Research, USDA Forest Service, Pacific Southwest Research Station.

Peterson, Russell. 2004. *The Pine Tree Book*, second edition. New York: Central Park Conservancy.

Presson, Art. Personal interview. May 24, 2011

——. E-mails to author. May 19, 2011, October 25, 2011, October 27, 2011, April 26, 2012.

Primack, R. and Higuchi, H. (2007) "Climate Change and Cherry Tree Blossom Festivals in Japan." *Arnoldia* 65/2, 14-22.

Radermacher, Marian and Wolfgang. Personal interview. April 6, 2010.

Richman, Jeff. E-mails to author. October 25, 2011, October 27, 2011, April 26, 2012.

Rizick, Steven. Personal interview. June 8, 2011.

——. E-mail to author. April 30, 2012.

Roddick, Christopher. Caucasian Wingnut: Comments. Videorecording at http://v1.bbg.org/exp/bigtrees/audio.html.

——. E-mail to author. June 21, 2012.

Rogers, E. B. 1971. *The Forests and Wetlands of New York City*. Boston: Little, Brown.

Rombone, Ray. Personal interview. September 2, 2009.

Rosenstock, Bonnie. 2005. "Peter's Pear Tree Plaque Is Going Home at Last." *The Villager*, pp. 16–22.

Ross, Janet. Conversation. June 15, 2012.

Sanderson, Eric W. 2009. *Mannahatta: A Natural History of New York City*. New York: Harry N. Abrams.

———. Personal interview. February 24, 2012.

Scarpa, P., and Stelter, L. 2009. *Bay Ridge (Then & Now)*. For the Bay Ridge Historical Society: Arcadia Publishing.

Schama, Simon. 1995. *Landscape and Memory*. New York: Alfred A. Knopf.

Sebesta, L. 1999. "Balmville Tree: Living Landmark." *New York State Conservationist*.

Sheppard, P. R., and Cook, E. R. November 25, 1985. "Report to the Bronx Forest Project: Dendrochronology of the Eastern Hemlocks." Palisades, NY: Tree-Ring Laboratory, Lamont-Doherty Geological Observatory of Columbia University.

Sherman, Danya. E-mail to the author. April 17, 2011.

Snowden, Bruce. August 10, 2011. "Another Plaque to Honor Corlear Tree?" Letter to the Editor. *Riverdale Press*.

———. Personal interview. November 2, 2011.

Squitieri, C., Gurbo, V., and Azimov, N. 2008. "Yellow Fever in Bay Ridge." The Presence of the Past: Turning Points in NYC, at http://www.macaulay.cuny.edu/seminars/napoli08/index.php/Yellow_Fever_in_Bay_Ridge.

Sternberg, G., with Wilson, J. 2004. *Native Trees for North American Landscapes*. Portland, Oregon: The Timber Press.

Steyer, William. E-mail to Fiona Watt. April 14, 2008.

———. Telephone interview. April 24, 2012.

Supina, Robert. Personal interview. March 21, 2010.

Swett, B. 2000. *Great Trees of New York City: A Guide*. New York: New York Tree Trust.

"Sycamore Court Condos," at http://sycamorecourtcondos.com/index.asp. Accessed October 17, 2011.

"Washington Square New York City: History." 2011. Washington Square Association, Inc., and Friends of Washington Square Park. http://washingtonsquarenyc.org/washington_square_park_history.htm.

Watt, F. E-mails to the author. April 14, 2008, April 16, 2010, April 4, 2012.

———, and Wells, M. 2009. "Historic Trees: When to Preserve, When to Let go?" City Trees. Society of Municipal Arborists. http://www.urban-forestry.com/publications-city-trees.

———, Greenfeld, J., and Wells, M. Personal interview. April 30, 2010.

"Weeds Gone Wild: Alien Plant Invaders of Natural Areas." 2010. Plant Conservation Alliance, Alien Plant Working Group. www.nps.gov/plants/alien/.

Wells, Matthew. Personal interviews. May 6, 2009, May 11, 2011, June 5, 2012.

———. E-mails to the author. February 26, 2010, April 15, 2010, April 12, 2012.

White, N., and Willensky, E. 2000. *AIA Guide to New York City: The Classic Guide to New York's Architecture*, 4th edition. New York: Three Rivers Press.

Williams, C. 2002. André Michaux, a biographical sketch, at www.michaux.org.

Wright, T., and Katsuhiko, M. 1990. *Zen Gardens*. Kyoto: Mitsumura Suiko Shoin Co.

Index